With best wi

NO MORE POLITICS PLEASE!

A Pocket Guide to the Good Life
Politicians Promise But Never Deliver

Leonard Louis Brown

Illustrations by Chico Kidd

MINERVA PRESS
LONDON
MIAMI   RIO DE JANEIRO   DELHI

NO MORE POLITICS PLEASE!: *A Pocket Guide to the Good Life Politicians Promise But Never Deliver*
Copyright © Leonard Louis Brown 2000

ISBN 0 75411 563 1

First published 2000 by
MINERVA PRESS
315–317 Regent Street
London W1B 2HS

Printed in Great Britain for Minerva Press

NO MORE POLITICS PLEASE!

A Pocket Guide to the Good Life
Politicians Promise But Never Deliver

All living creatures, mankind included, instinctively believe that the environment into which they are born is as it should be and that one must therefore do the best one can do for oneself, no matter how this may affect others.

This remained true until twentieth-century technology transformed a world of chronic shortages in all good things into one of potential abundance and thus made possible an even greater advance.

We could now have real democracy for the first time ever. Government by the people without politicians and political corruption is now ours for the taking, if secrecy is outlawed and all information about all things is freely available.

A new generation, properly educated, would then know how to exploit technology wisely and efficiently for the benefit of all living creatures and so create a near Utopia in a few decades.

This book is the first to explain, simply, clearly and indisputably:

Why we could now properly feed, educate, house, clothe and care for every normal person on this planet, if our affairs were honestly and efficiently managed.

Why all present-day democracies are not democratic, despite their pretensions, why politics is inherently and incurably corrupt, and why we could now dispense with politics and have real democracy, if we are prepared to outlaw secrecy.

Why we could then restore the environment and put an end to war, terrorism and munitions production.

Why all normal people could be well educated and cultured, why there need be no enforced poverty, fraud or organised crime and why narcotics addiction, religious bigotry and widespread ignorance would cease.

Why 'fat cats', politicians, fraudulent statistics and spin doctors would no longer be tolerated and why all man-made problems would be remedied as and when they occurred.

All that is needed to get the ball rolling is to find sufficient time to absorb the facts revealed in this book and spread the word. Good sense would then to the rest.

Contents

Dear Mike,

I have had contact some months past with Mr Len Brown, a retired industrialist who worked in high technology, lives in London but is now moving to Bournemouth. He is the author of a book to which he has devoted a great deal of time and effort. He began with a study of what has been termed the English Disease but went on to study the crisis which faces the world as a whole. He is impressed with the contrast which exists between a rapidly progressing technology and a static or retrogressive situation in human affairs. He thus analyses our current failure in government, administration, economics, education, communication and thought, showing where we have gone wrong and how we can escape from our present deadlock. This could be a work of great importance and it is one to which I have promised to add an introduction.[1] It seems to me, moreover, a book which might appear for people at the right time, a work with a hopeful message for people who may be tempted to despair. Our problems, he urges, are not insoluble. They can be solved if we tackle them in the right way.

He will contact you himself but I am writing in advance to assure you that his work deserves careful consideration and that a publisher might well be found for a work which may attract attention and might indeed prove influential in the years to come.

With good wishes,
Yours ever,
Cyril
(letter to Cyril Parkinson's literary agent, April 1986)

---

[1] Unfortunately. Cyril Parkinson could not, as promised, provide an introduction to this book as, sadly, he died in 1990.

ACKNOWLEDGEMENTS

This book could not have been written without the invaluable help of the late Cyril Northcote Parkinson, celebrated author, historian, and man of many parts. We moved in entirely different circles and met by a strange accident when I had given up all hope of completing this work. He listened to what I had to say and inspired me to continue.

Chico Kidd, to whom I was introduced by a fellow bridge player, is another without whose encouragement and contribution this work would have come to nothing. She thought I was crazy when I first tried to explain what I had in mind, but soon came round to my way of thinking.

But most of all is owed to my darling wife, Mathilda, a remarkable, kind and modest woman of many parts. Perfect mother, equal partner in all our business affairs and companion in our extensive travels in many countries, she has been and remains an inspiration and tower of strength.

Writing a book of this kind does not go well with industry, commerce and home life. Producing the necessities of life, as I have had to do all my working life to make a decent living leaves so little time to think about other things that this book's many important conclusions could not have been reached, had I not been an insomniac since childhood. But every achievement has its price. Being married to an insomniac obsessed with a mission is not the proverbial bed of roses. And yet no two people could be more devoted to each other despite our having such heavy commitments that the best we could do to celebrate our recent sixtieth wedding anniversary was spend a very quiet and private weekend in a nearby resort. The many sacrifices entailed in completing this work would be repaid ten billion times or more if it encourages enough people to observe carefully what is going on around them and think more deeply.

They would then realise that human predators could not rob, cheat, mislead and enslave us in a genuine democracy. Hiding information of any kind that could affect other people would be so heavily penalised that the potential gain would not be worthwhile. Working together for mutual benefit would become a habit. Elderly people in genuine democracies will see things differently. Optimism will be the order of the day.

PREFACE

That so many elderly British people one meets nowadays say they would not wish to be born in today's corrupt society is a sad reflection on our present-day way of life that can be expressed only with the benefit of hindsight. Youngsters cannot see things as they are because every generation is brought up to believe that everything is as it should be and that human nature prevents change for the better.

This was true in the past, but is true no longer. Technology is now so advanced that given time and understanding of what needs to be done we could produce all the resources needed to give the entire population of this planet a good education and constantly improving living standards, health and quality of life in a pollution-free environment.

People would no longer need to leave their homeland, family, relatives and friends to escape grinding poverty, degradation, persecution or other injustice. Everyone would be doing their best to make the world a better place in which to live and bring up children. The refugee problem and most others that now afflict us would become the kind of history that does not repeat itself.

All that's needed is to manage our affairs honestly and efficiently.

Every nation's workforce would be equipped with the skills required to produce the goods and services that contribute most to living standards, good health and quality of life, and to do all this efficiently and economically. Only those unfit for work would be unemployed. All activities would combine to create a near perfect balance in all things, as applies throughout the universe.

This is in stark contrast to the present situation. Government policies everywhere are creating a rapidly increasing imbalance, the intended outcome of which will be such chaos that the only escape will be ruthless Big Brother societies. Life for nearly everyone is immeasurably worse than it should be and worsens almost daily without this being noticed. We are, instead, told how lucky we are to have living standards so much higher than in bygone days. That our living standards and quality of life should be immeasurably better and that every able-bodied person should be well educated, usefully employed, generously paid and well equipped to make good use of constantly increasing leisure is carefully concealed.

It would be no exaggeration to suggest that all but a relative handful of people are either inefficiently and wastefully employed, unemployed, prematurely retired or unfit for work. The vast majority of jobs provide services that serve only to make easy profits and distract attention from the harsh realities of life. If human nature is responsible, it is that of our rulers, not of those they govern.

But before taking this further, we must know what we are talking about. Wealth in this book is defined as 'any resource that can improve living standards and/or quality of life'. Waste is 'any productive activity that does not make its proper contribution to the creation of wealth'. If these definitions are agreed, then waste in Britain, for example, is more than 95 per cent. Most other countries are more prudent, but waste is fast growing everywhere.

Typical of this waste is the proliferation of charities, societies, institutions and pressure groups soliciting donations. Vast sums are spent to persuade us that it is our duty to give as much as or more than we can afford to alleviate, cure, prevent or improve a growing catalogue of social, medical, economic, political and other problems or activities. Some mean well. Others do much more harm than good. Far too many do little more than promote the false images and reputations that win fame and fortune in a world driven mad by uncontrolled market forces and unbridled commercialism. Charities and other appeals for help would not be needed if the money donated was used to promote genuine democracy.

We have yet to learn that we are trapped in a system of government that has purposely been made so complex and incomprehensible that more problems are created than can be resolved. These, in turn, spawn more charities, pressure groups and other organisations, increasing still further the demand on shrinking resources without the faintest hope of fulfilling their promises.

All is part of a vicious spiral of multiplying problems and corresponding increases in paid staff and other expenses. It should be obvious to those who study and comment on current affairs and influence public opinion that nothing can be resolved in isolation.

This appalling mess is not the accident it is made to appear, but matters are so arranged that we are too busy or distracted to observe and think matters through deeply enough to see things as they are rather than as our leaders and their acolytes would have us believe. Contrary to what we are told, the insoluble problems that continue to plague us are the inevitable product of an obsolete system of government and economic and social management that cannot exploit fast-changing technology for the benefit of the electorate. To make matters worse, it is increasingly corrupt and inefficient. It should be obvious that civilised coexistence will end, unless ways and means are found to remedy this situation and resolve all man-made problems as and when they arise. They would be rare and easily dealt with, were our affairs managed honestly and efficiently.

Incredibly fast-developing technology has destroyed all

limits to productivity. It also provides the tools needed to transform bogus democracy into the genuine article. Government by the people for the benefit of all the people is now ours for the taking, but only if secrecy is outlawed and if all knowledge about all things and all people is freely available. The only exception would be genuinely private matters that cannot harm or help others. The resulting abundance of useful resources would speedily resolve all long-standing problems. Fresh problems would easily be dealt with as and when they arise.

A transition so far-reaching takes time, but once the mechanisms are in place and initial bugs are eliminated, a near Utopia could be created within a few decades. Constant improvement would be the aim in all activities.

By far the most valuable of all resources is a properly educated population. We cannot otherwise have genuine democracy, with all that this implies. Constantly improving education would foster personal responsibility and collaboration, improve public health and behaviour, increase the efficiency of technology and make life better and better. A little-known fact of life is that everything generates more of its own kind, be it good, bad or indifferent.

The potential benefits of genuine democracy are too many and too far-reaching to be visualised at present. But, on the other hand, the dreadful alternative is unthinkable. There is really no choice. Our very survival hangs on our decision.

Unless we accept both the constraints and the responsibilities called for by genuine democracy, our children's children will inherit a world of harsh, ignorant Big Brother societies of the kind forecast by George Orwell. The alternative would be a planet made uninhabitable for millions of years.

At the root of all our problems is the unavoidable waste of a system that has served its original purpose as best it can and outlived its usefulness. Whereas non-productive paid workers were relatively few in the past, the greater majority of the nation's workers now produce little or nothing of real value to society. Fewer and fewer produce the necessities and worthwhile luxuries that could be had by even the poorest paid workers in a genuine democracy. Insult is added to injury by top parasites giving themselves hundreds or thousands of times more than is earned by workers who produce or provide the products and services we need most. Present-day extremes of wealth and poverty are obscene.

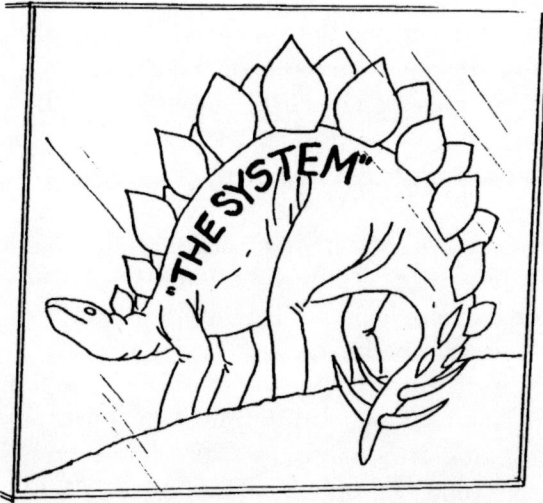

IT OUTLIVED ITS USEFULNESS

This devil's brew is made more threatening by vast quantities of weapons of destruction that should no longer be needed, but which are extremely profitable and help maintain the status quo. Fictitious foreign enemies are therefore invented to justify this waste, which in turn compels more and more industrialised nations to produce munitions in a never-ending vicious spiral. Nothing could be more diabolical, no hypocrisy could be greater.

Our real enemies are the backroom people who control world finances, international affairs, international trade and all other influential institutions. They are also our real rulers. They pre-select, train and finance our leaders, all of whom must do as they are told or return to obscurity. We now vote for live, well-trained puppets who pretend to be in charge and would have us believe they are doing their best in conditions that make it impossible to do better.

The greater and still increasing part of the entire wealth of the world now goes into fewer and fewer pockets. All populations are being pauperised amidst bogus claims that economies are booming, but everyone is too confused and misinformed to realise what is happening.

All this must and can be changed, but having the tools of democracy is not enough. The abolition of secrecy in all matters that can affect the welfare of other people is equally indispensable. Genuine democracy can function and flourish only when truth is standard practice, when all knowledge about all things is freely available, and when the greater majority of the people are sufficiently well educated to put that knowledge to good use.

Secrecy, if the truth be known, is essential only to criminals, politicians, currency and commodity speculators and all others who undermine society. Only idiots would want secrecy, if we knew how much would be gained by complete openness in all matters that could affect other people.

The production of wealth would be multiplied fivefold or more. Research would be directed towards producing the things we need most. All the known facts of a given issue could be presented to the electorate, thus making it easy to reach the best possible decisions for the majority and compensate fairly those who may be disadvantaged. Perfect solutions are not of this world.

With things as they are, we are told only what our leaders want us to know, which in turn is based on part or fractional truths used cleverly to hide those that really matter. Part-truths are the most effective and damaging of all lies.

The Middle East conflict is a prime example. The root cause is not religion or land or refugees or Jerusalem. It is the ownership by oil sheikhs and other powerful vested interests of immense oil resources that should belong to the people, as would all natural resources in a democratic world. Feudalism, mass ignorance and oppression, enforced by massive supplies of munitions, enable them to retain their unlawful possessions. And so they foment hatred for a newly created nearby nation that practises a form of democracy and threatens their cruel status quo.

SECRECY

Misrepresenting crucial facts is standard practice in all such matters, politics most of all. Its purpose is to win power, regardless of the potential damage to society. Its lifeblood is secrecy, as in all criminal activities. Politicians have no place in an open society. Nor could there be corruption, profiteering, overcharging, inefficiency, organised crime, widespread ignorance, or excessive waste of any other kind. Human predators would be easily identified and rendered helpless.

The world can never be perfect. But we can and will have one that is constantly improving, a concept so foreign to our teaching and upbringing that it must be repeated time and time again.

Getting this message across in simple language is the purpose of a book that has taken twenty-seven years of thinking, writing, rewriting and interminable discussions and arguments with friends and acquaintances, only one of whom could see what I was hoping to achieve. My meeting that man was one of an astonishing sequence of strange coincidences that shaped my life, made this book possible, and convinced me everything that whatever we do is predestined, that nothing can happen before its time, and that nothing can stop something happening when its time arrives.

Final proof is that it would have served no purpose to publish this book sooner. The climate of public opinion had to change. Only during the past few years have the unseen objectives of world leaders become apparent to those of us with the time and inclination to ponder such matters.

Only now is it increasingly obvious that fewer and fewer have job security, even in banking or teaching or other traditionally secure professions or trades.

Only with hindsight can one see that every generation everywhere is worse educated than its predecessor.

Only now are people beginning to realise that doctors and pharmaceutical manufacturers have a lot to answer for and that government agencies are responsible for Aids, mad cow disease and other major disasters.

Only now can we see that narcotics addiction cannot be ended by enforcement agencies and that drug barons are above the law.

Only now are people waking up to the fact that poisons

used in factory farming to control pests are deadly health hazards and that the future lies in organic farming.

Only now is there a growing appreciation of the superiority of natural prevention and natural remedies over synthetic substitutes and of the long-term deadly side effects of so-called miracle drugs and inoculations with animal-based vaccines.

Only now is it obvious that people go into politics to make themselves rich and powerful and that the bureaucracy, as we know it, represents the greatest of all dangers to

THE NEW ELITE

freedom.

Only now are people questioning the systematic destruction of essential manufacturing industries and the loudly claimed merits of global markets.

Only now is there a growing awareness of the inherent fraud of government claims and statistics.

Only now are people beginning to question the huge salaries of footballers and other sports people, the obscene rewards of entertainers and other non-producers, and the multimillion pound bonuses of bankers and other wheeler dealers who produce so little of real value to the masses.

The lesson to be learned from all this is that the football hooligans, the layabouts, the dependants on social security, the unmarried juvenile mothers, the petty thieves, the drug addicts, the alcoholics, the multiplying suicides, are nearly all victims of the system. Very few can be fairly blamed. Had they had the good fortune to be educated properly and brought up in an environment that makes life worth living, they would be rational, cultured and full of useful knowledge. In short, the world would be a very different place. Such a world could now be created for the first time ever in the evolution of mankind.

TIME FOR CHANGE

POLITICS DON'T CHANGE VERY MUCH

If socialism is a society in which technology is efficiently exploited for the benefit of the entire population, and in which wages, salaries, bonuses and other rewards are proportional to the contribution one makes to society, then its father must surely be the little-known Georgy V Plenkhanov (1856–1918).

A prominent revolutionary, idealist and contemporary of Lenin whom he denounced as a monomaniac, Plenkhanov was well aware of the corrupting influence of power and knew that a revolution imposed on an ignorant proletariat would result in a much worse form of despotism. He warned that even the most dedicated leaders would inevitably become tyrants, and that injustice, ignorance, poverty, war and other man-made evils can be ended only by a peaceful revolution that is initiated and carried out by the masses. But he also made it clear that the masses must be sufficiently educated to know what changes are needed and how to bring them about, and that the economy must be able to produce the resources needed to satisfy all their legitimate demands. The revolution would otherwise fail.

This was idealism only because it was ahead of its time. The just society he had in mind, namely real democracy, cannot function without immensely powerful computers and international electronic communications. Nor can sufficient resources be produced until technology destroys all boundaries to productivity. We have the computers, communications and technology, but we do not yet have a suitably educated population. Nor can people who are indoctrinated from birth with misguided or fraudulent beliefs acquire this knowledge or use knowledge wisely. There's truth in the old saying: 'Old dogs can't be taught new tricks.' Learning how to use technology wisely in a fast-changing world must be taught from infancy, and is why the transition to real democracy will take several decades to complete.

This will happen despite all appearances to the contrary, being part of an ongoing process of evolution. All knowledge exists from time immemorial and is merely waiting to be discovered. New knowledge surfaces when experience reaches a certain level, at which time nothing can prevent new knowledge being used and translated into action. In short, nothing can change before its time, but nothing can prevent change when the time for change arrives.

Many people will be inconvenienced in the initial stages, but given the enormity of the prize (the benefits cannot be pictured in our present dog-eat-dog environment) this would be the biggest economic and social bargain of all time.

I beg you, readers, therefore, not to be misled by the size of this book. It has taken many years to express so many crucial truths so concisely and comprehensibly. No matter who you are, or how little or how much you know, or how deep-rooted your indoctrination, it will hopefully give you considerable food for thought and convince you that life for future generations can and will be immeasurably better than you could have imagined in your wildest dreams. This crucial message must somehow be conveyed to every normal man, woman and child on this planet.

APPEARANCES CAN BE DECEPTIVE

Never before was there so much disillusion about politics and politicians, so much foreboding about the future, so little understanding of what needs to be done to remedy the situation. And yet no generation was ever so privileged, did we but know it.

The outlook would be very different if we could see things as they are rather than as our leaders make them

MEDIAEVAL VOTING ...

appear. We humans have acquired only a tiny fraction of the knowledge that will eventually be discovered, but if one thing is certain it is that we will never know how the universe was created or why.

It is reasonable to suppose that there is a purpose in all things, but whatever the purpose for creating mankind, it cannot be to make a privileged few immensely wealthy at the expense of the masses. Nor can it be to have girls lining up for intercourse with over-sexed presidents or other celebrities, or for people to be criminals, football hooligans, alcoholics or narcotics addicts, or for the masses to be robbed by currency and commodity speculators or greedy distributors.

The answer, if good sense is our guide, lies in the work-

MODERN VOTING

ings of a natural environment. Like it or not, we are as much a part of it and controlled by it as all other species, despite our superior intelligence, dexterity and mobility.

All living creatures in the wild can use any of the available natural resources. The lords of the jungle have no patents, copyright, land titles or other exclusive rights. The theory and practice of economics in natural environments are expressed in one simple sentence, namely one can have only that which has been produced. From the moment they are born, infants begin to learn how to develop fully their inherent talents and make the best of what they have. Experience is transformed into habit.

Every living thing in the wild is food for other forms of life, but animals rarely prey on their own kind. Scavengers keep the environment clean by recycling unavoidable waste and are the fewest needed to do the job. There are no politicians or power struggles. The past does not dictate the future. Everything combines to create and preserve a balance in all things. Temporary disasters are repaired as soon as circumstances allow. Nothing is wasted. Everything is recycled.

Our ways are entirely different. We would otherwise realise that this generation has inherited a world that in less than a normal lifespan was transformed from one of unavoidable shortages in almost everything needed for a good life into one of potential abundance, subject only to one precondition. The principles of nature must apply in all things, including the ownership and exploitation of natural resources. Human nature would then do the rest.

Impossible though this may seem at this moment in time, a near Utopia could be created in a few decades, having made which observations we can embark on a short, but hopefully enlightening voyage of discovery, beginning with an imaginary, but well-merited, trial of world leaders.

THE TRIAL AND VERDICT

'Members of the jury, have you considered your verdict?'

'Yes, your lordship.'

'Do you find the accused guilty or not guilty?'

'Guilty, your honour, but we have reservations about certain aspects of these proceedings and request your permission to voice them before you pronounce sentence.'

'Ladies and gentlemen, you are adjudicating in this most important of all public trials because you are leaders in your chosen occupations, are noted for your integrity and ability, and collectively speak with authority for the world's most important trades and professions. Any contribution is therefore welcome. Please state what have you in mind.'

'Your lordship, the evidence compels us to find the accused guilty of the worst crimes ever perpetrated against humanity. Hundreds of millions of innocent people were slaughtered, maimed, starved, tortured, robbed or imprisoned for no other reason than that they happened to be where they were at the time. But although these crimes make news and history, they are the lesser part of the cruelty and suffering inflicted on mankind. Far greater is the deliberate creation of uneducated, mindless and increasingly frustrated populations and a near total waste of our most valuable resources. This greatest of all crimes goes unnoticed because everything conspires to conceal the truth and present false pictures.

'It is now known that every normal child has enormous potential for absorbing knowledge and contributing to human progress. If therefore all children were properly edu-

cated, there would be so many more talented, responsible, and productive people than there are now that the obscene pay differentials that are increasingly commonplace and still widening could no longer be justified. The highest annual earnings could not be more than five or six times the lowest, but the poorest workers would be wealthy by present-day standards.

'Very few children can presently develop their inherent talent. They are taught less and less about the truly important things in life and brought up to believe that their every wish must be instantly gratified. More and more leave school unable to read or write properly or do simple sums. Very few can distinguish right from wrong. They make gods of the brash and the trash. They have no sense of value.

'And so those who can hit or kick a ball harder or more accurately than other ball hitters or kickers can earn more in

a week than skilled factory and farm workers can earn in several years. A screen star can command ten million dollars or more to play a role in a film that serves only to distract attention from the harsh failings of the present system. The Bill Gateses of today's world become billionaires by exploiting knowledge that should be free for all to use without charge. The legalised theft of billions of dollars by large-scale currency and commodity speculators, such as George Soros, is viewed as an honourable way to make a living. Sons of prime ministers can become sterling millionaires for selling weapons of destruction in a world driven mad by commercial pressures. There is no end to a saga of obscene wastes that deny world populations their rightful heritage.

'The accused have known for many years that government by the people for the benefit of the entire population would be feasible when computers and electronic communications are sufficiently developed and that this would put an end to the immense waste that is presently inherent in all activities. Suitable preparations for this peaceful revolution would be well advanced by now, were our affairs managed honestly and efficiently.

'And yet we all agree that two crucial questions are left unanswered. Firstly, to what extent were the accused free agents? Secondly, would we behave differently had we had the same upbringing, opportunities and temptations? Power corrupts even saints.

'The reality, your lordship, is that we are presently locked into a system, rightly described by the great wartime leader Winston Churchill as "the best we could have at the time", but which we now know has served its purpose and is obsolete. We respectfully suggest that the accused should be severely punished only if they try to maintain the status quo and so retain their power and immense privilege.'

'I take note of what you say, ladies and gentlemen of the jury, and thank you on behalf of the people for the tremendous service you have rendered mankind. These proceedings could not take place or be concluded successfully without your willing co-operation. Your persistence, patience and disregard of deadly threats to you and to your respective families from our hitherto all-powerful leaders will command the eternal gratitude of future generations.

'The evidence we have heard has exposed the corruption that now permeates every function of daily life and exposed the hidden network of international connections and secret deals that enable unseen power mongers to manipulate government policies.

'Rumours of an all-powerful secret group who control world affairs were common currency for centuries. Like most other people, I discounted them until mounting evidence proved they were completely true. It is now known that a group, known as the *"Bilderbergers"*, comprising of leading bankers, industrialists, academics and politicians meet periodically in heavily guarded hotels or private resorts and in conditions of absolute secrecy. John Pilcher drew attention to their plans in *Hidden Agendas*. Des Griffin researched their origin and named several prominent members in *The Fourth Reich of the Rich*, but nothing was disclosed about the way they operate.

'It is now known that they select, recruit, finance and train future leaders in politics, education, industry and other important establishments and that those who make the grade must do as they are told. This is why it makes virtually no difference which party is in power. Among their recent invitees were British Liberal Party leader Paddy Ashdown in 1989, Tory Chancellor of the Exchequer Kenneth Clarke in 1993, World Bank boss James Wolfensohn and socialist British finance minister Gordon Brown in June 1999 (*Daily Telegraph* and *Financial Times*). His colleague Peter Mandelson also attended this meeting (*Private Eye*, 20 August 1999).

'Candidates for top jobs know that the privilege, invaluable connections and wealth that are reserved for power holders cannot be had in any other walk of life, no matter how talented one may be, and that these can be had only if they maintain the status quo. Democracy, as presently practised, is the very reverse of what it pretends to be. Exposing what amounts to an almost unbelievable conspiracy and showing where ultimate power really lies has opened the door to a world of peace and plenty that very few believed was possible until now.

'It is, however, extremely difficult to accept that many of the so-called "truths" we are taught from infancy are wrong, least of all that human nature is unchangeable and responsible for all our problems and that nothing can be done to change the system. This hurdle must be overcome and the real truth made widely known. The new and immeasurably better life that technology makes available is otherwise unobtainable. The following little-known realities should help put such matters into better perspective.

'All knowledge has existed since the beginning of time. Nothing is invented in the true sense of the word. New facts come to light when experience reaches a certain level, at which time any number of people may be thinking along the same lines. The one who first publishes or applies for a patent or employs a better lawyer is the "inventor". All is part of an ongoing evolutionary process of development in which nothing can happen before its time, but in which nothing can prevent a change when its time arrives.

'Knowledge often surfaces long before it can be used. Democracy was invented by ancient Greeks 2,500 years before the necessary computers and electronic communications were developed and before the masses could be appropriately educated. We must also adjust our thinking to this new way of life, as becomes clear if we examine the nature and purpose of government.

'A nation's government affects every person in the country and is best described as "management on the grandest scale". Managers are employed to make the best possible decisions, to do which they must have access to all the relevant information. Nothing that can influence their decisions may be concealed.

'The people make all decisions in a genuine democracy. It follows that these will be best for the majority only if secrecy is prohibited in all matters that can affect the people and if infringements are heavily punished. All the known information about all people and all things could then be stored in computerised information centres, regularly updated and accessed through home modems.

'But the drastic changes called for in the way we think and behave and conduct our affairs would put our leaders out of business. We are therefore persuaded to believe that to prohibit secrecy is an infringement of human rights.

'Nothing could be more fraudulent. The free exchange of all knowledge and information, other than harmless private matters, is the next giant leap forward in mankind's evolution. Our attitude to water shows why there should be nothing to hide when everything needed for a good life is readily available.

'People with water on tap rarely give it a thought – until there is a shortage. They quickly forget the inconvenience when the supply is restored.

'But murder has been committed for a drink of water in an arid desert. Nor is this confined to life and death matters. Some people will go to any lengths to get what they want.

'Shortages of one kind or another are at the root of all problems. Promises to resolve problems by spending more money may win elections. More productivity is the only cure. Abundance and fair shares provide the solution to all problems faced by government, but this demands total change in human motivation, the purpose of every enterprise, the practice of economics, and the way nations manage their economy and trade with other nations.

'All who are assembled in this courtroom have witnessed the greatest single advance in human evolution since ancient man emerged from a primeval forest and harnessed fire and discovered the wheel. Technology multiplied several million times in a few decades and destroyed all limits to productivity. A world of unavoidable shortages was transformed into one of potential abundance. And so, ladies and gentlemen, the question to be asked is: "Why are we not producing these resources, now that we have the means?"

'It is because an incredible waste of resources is unavoidable when the ultimate aim of those who manage our affairs is to retain power, and when monetary profit is the motivation in everything we do, regardless of the harm this may inflict on the nation. Parasites in a natural environment increase the supply of useful resources by keeping the environment clean and are the fewest required to do this. Human parasites proliferate and consume or destroy more useful resources than the economy can produce.

'Democracy would transform the situation. Everything is open to public inspection. Monetary profit is no longer the driving force in all things. Destructive commercial pressures disappear. Profit is measured by the gain in human betterment, as judged by independent assessors. Constantly improving education is the first priority.

'The result would be an efficient, diversified economy that can produce the goods and services required to give everyone a good life, protect the environment and maintain and increase the value of the nation's industries and infrastructure. Efficiency experts would regularly monitor all productive activities and compare them with others of their kind. The free exchange of all information about all things would make it easy to constantly improve the efficiency and quality of manufactures and services, lower costs and reduce waste. All the services required to achieve maximum productivity and constantly improving quality would be provided free of charge.

'Given good government, we could now produce an abundance of whatever is needed to give every normal person on this planet a good life. Moreover, the pace of developing technology increases daily, creating a situation in which a peaceful, increasingly prosperous world with constantly improving quality of life for the entire population could be had within a few decades.

'There will come a time when everything needed could be produced in a working week of twenty hours or less, but what would be the point – if the time saved is spent watching TV, or shopping, or getting drunk, or taking drugs, or going on the rampage? Better ways would be found to use increased leisure.

'There is unlimited scope for active participation in sports, music, theatre, ballet, opera and a host of other worthwhile hobbies and cultural pursuits. Essential social services, that cannot presently be afforded, would be provided as a duty and without pay. But there are five major obstacles.

'First is our belief that the inherent greed of human nature is responsible for all our problems. Experience proves that human nature, properly motivated, can perform miracles.

'Second is the fact that overpaid workers create underpaid workers. People should be paid only what they are worth.

'Third is that we can have only that which we produce. If people are unemployed, produce trash, provide unwanted services, or make weapons of destruction, then they cannot produce the things that make life better.

'Fourth is the difficulty of noticing slowly worsening conditions until it is too late to remedy the situation. This is well illustrated by putting frogs in a pail of cold water out of which they can jump whenever they choose. If the water is heated very gradually they will boil to death.

'Last and most formidable is the secrecy that creates an environment in which the people cannot tell right from wrong, good from bad, true from false, honest from corrupt, and in which nearly every human activity is valued by the amount of monetary profit it can make. The result is war and mass atrocities, growing crime, infinite damage to society and the environment, and an astronomical waste of human and other resources. If the word waste is properly defined, it accounts for more than 95 per cent of the potential for producing useful resources in Britain and the USA. Just imagine what life could be like if only half that potential is realised!

'By contrast, when all things are open and above board and when all knowledge is freely available, it is easy to see things as they are and act accordingly. The potential for human endeavour is then limitless. Living standards, quality of life and the environment would all improve faster and faster in line with developing technology. War, poverty,

CALLING PEOPLE ANIMALS

INSULTS THE ANIMALS

exploitation, extortion, enforced ignorance, massive waste and all other crimes against humanity would be confined to history.

'But despite the enormity of change demanded by the transition to democracy, very few people would be seriously hurt or inconvenienced. Even the wealthiest people could retain more than enough of their possessions to maintain superb living standards. Their quality of life would be immeasurably better. Bodyguards and immensely expensive security installations would no longer be needed. They could mix freely and anonymously, go wherever they choose and behave like normal people, subject only to their accepting the transition with good grace. Having made which observations, ladies and gentlemen, we will adjourn the proceedings.'

REALITIES OF A CHANGING WORLD

This imaginary trial of world leaders was not inspired by investigations into the misuse of donations and wrongful acceptance of gifts by top politicians and presidents in Britain, Germany, France and Israel among others. These are 'political window dressing' to create the impression that politics is honest and to divert public attention from the worst of all crimes against humanity.

It is intended to draw attention to the reality of politics and power, to the almost unbelievable waste generated by our present system of government and economic and social management, and to the infinite potential of technology if it is used wisely in a completely open society.

Whereas every activity controlled by government does the very reverse of what it claims to do, all functions in a real democracy would work for the benefit of all the people. Words would mean what they say. Actions would fulfil promises. Power could no longer corrupt, because it would belong to the people and would be spread as evenly among them as possible.

A comparison with the present system of government should show the potential.

Politicians are elected on promises to do what is best for the nation, with matters so arranged that they can obtain all the facts and advice needed to make the best possible decisions. But politics must be divisive because it is all about gaining and retaining power. Conflicting vested interests are its lifeblood. What matters most is winning the next election.

Good government would unite the people by giving them a common purpose.

British politicians are best judged by the fact that whereas it took several centuries to complete the decline and fall of the Roman Empire, they lost a far greater and more powerful empire in thirty years. They then compounded the crime by destroying the vital manufacturing industries that produce the things we need most and gave themselves the nation's highest honours and rewards for achievement. Beat that if you can!

They travel in heavily guarded convoys or by private planes and helicopters. They stay in presidential suites that can cost fifty times more than normal rooms. They wine and dine free on the finest and best that only the wealthiest can afford. They can acquire expensive homes at a fraction of their market value. Free holidays in superb locations for their family and close friends are theirs for the asking. They have access to invaluable inside information that taxpayers cannot get at any price. Their children can have the best education available. They earn immense fees and royalties from journalism and autobiographies.

Who can now pretend that crime does not pay? Successive generations of political families and their cronies have first choice of the best, least demanding (and excessively paid) jobs in public and privatised services and industries. Politicians in so-called 'liberated colonies' can hijack the entire national economy! Billions of US dollars and other currencies are stashed away in secret bank accounts.

Is it any wonder that politicians want things to stay as they are?

Or that bureaucrats and other government officials have joined the gravy train?

Or that the economists they employ compile fraudulent statistics?

Or that privileged leaders in professions and the obscenely overpaid sports people, entertainers, speculators, fat cats and other parasites will do everything possible to perpetuate the present system?

The fundamental question to be answered, therefore, is: 'How can we change the system and eliminate this colossal waste?'

Despite all appearances to the contrary, the transition to real democracy would be much easier than was winning the last war, but it requires time, patience and a widespread public understanding of a number of important but little-known economic and social realities and issues. The changes that must be made in the way we conduct our affairs would then be self-evident.

It must be clearly understood, however, that although there are no political parties or politics in a real democracy, the present system can and must be used to change the system. A bloody revolution is not the answer. Change for the better can be brought about only by the will of the people, even though very few of those who initiate the transition will live to see it completed.

The instrument will be a new non-political party, dedicated to establishing real democracy, which would automatically be dissolved when democracy is installed and working. All seats in general elections would be contested until a sufficient majority has been won to complete the task.

The new party's election manifesto would explain why real democracy is the only system that is guaranteed to give children and future generations a secure and happy future, setting out in detail what needs to be done. The electorate would be warned that it may take fifteen years or more to make the changes and that this must not be interrupted by periodical elections unless the situation so demands.

It would also be made clear that improvement will be slow until the new system is fully operational and that the full benefits will not materialise for up to fifty years. As must be stated and restated time and again, real democracy cannot function properly until a new generation has been properly educated and outdated beliefs and practices are consigned to history books.

Secrecy in all matters affecting the nation would immediately be banned and heavily penalised. The electorate could then see all that is going on. The transition could be halted and a fresh start made, should things get out of hand.

Prospective candidates for seats in the transition government would need to have industrial or other appropriate experience and would be required to take written and oral exams to prove their competence and good sense, this being the most important of all skills. They would also undertake to support all promised reforms, but without restricting opinions or proposals. They would then be chosen by lottery to serve for five years. One-fifth would be replaced annually by similarly chosen officials and return to the non-government sector. There would be no more bureaucratic empire building and old boys' networks. Efficiency would be mandatory and continuously monitored in all public and private functions, services and industries.

Growing disillusion with the present system would guarantee ample funds and an abundance of willing and competent helpers, all of whom would know that a secretive and corrupt society cannot be made increasingly self-regulating, completely open and transparently honest overnight and that no system will change of its own accord.

The transition will initially require the services of at least as many administrators as are now employed, but whereas every new measure in the present system creates more paperwork and more regulators, the reverse would apply. Redundant officials would be retrained and transferred to the non-government sector without losing pay, status or pension rights. The five-year limit would apply to all government appointments and managers in public services.

The transition has much in common with space satellites. Launched by a sequence of modules, each falls away when its job is done, leaving the satellite to function with minimum controls from base. This principle of scrapping jobs when they have fulfilled their purpose would apply to all functions of daily life, because openness encourages everyone to become increasingly responsible for whatever they do. Everything would become increasingly self-regulating, with fewer and fewer rules, regulations and administrators. There can never be a Utopia, but we can and will have a society that is constantly improving.

The inevitable reaction to drastic proposals of this kind is that they are totally impractical because they must take too long to fulfil. Nothing could be more mistaken. Those who think in terms of centuries should be reminded of what happened during and after the last war. Nearly two-thirds of Britain's entire workforce became military personnel or war workers for the duration. A working knowledge of machines and processes was acquired in weeks or months that took years in peacetime. When war ended, demobbed soldiers, sailors, airmen and civilians resumed their old jobs or found new ones. Devastated cities were gradually restored, albeit much more slowly than in any other European country. New industries mushroomed and flourished until they were undermined by politicians. War's dreadful anxieties were set aside. And yet all this is insignificant, compared with the changes that took place in post-war Germany and Japan.

The enormity of the work required to restore post-war Germany defies imagination. Any one of several cities suffered more destruction than the whole of Britain. The world's most reputable 'experts' said it could not be repaired in a hundred years. Russia made doubly sure by stripping occupied territories of industrial machines and equipment and transporting German scientists and technologists to Soviet laboratories, factories and labour camps. America, Britain and France seized important patents and know-how and recruited many top brains for their own industries.

Most damage was restored within ten years, showing how wrong the 'experts' can be. Millions of professionals did muscle-breaking jobs for little or no pay. Ten years more saw West Germany's bombed cities and towns rebuilt better than before. West Germany was once again Europe's leading industrial nation. Victorious Britain fell far behind, despite the fact that Britain had more American aid than Germany.

So much for expert opinion!

Japan provides an even more striking example of man's potential. 'Backward' by Western standards and with two major cities devastated by nuclear weapons, they now have the strongest of all economies and currencies and the largest per capita genuine gross national product. Japanese workers are among the world's top earners, but professional and executive salaries are low by Western standards.

They have the best education and the least crime. Things

are deteriorating, as elsewhere, but anyone can still walk the streets of any city, town or village without fear of being robbed, mugged or raped. A rumoured higher suicide rate than in the Western world is not supported by statistics. The market value of Japanese stock exchange equities exceeds that of the entire Common Market. No one knows how much real estate they own throughout the world. The once despised copycat is now world leader in every branch of high technology to which the nation applies its collective talent, effort and drive to make things better.

The Germans and Japanese achieved these miracles in less than thirty years, since when technology has multiplied tenfold or more. Twice as much could now be achieved in half the time, but let us not forget that all nations are targeted victims of the conspirators. The Germans, Japanese and other seemingly prosperous nations are all being systematically corrupted and dumbed down.

Cynics who declare that this transition cannot possibly happen, and who quote the failure of previous revolutions to justify this misguided opinion, have got it all wrong. They failed because no better system was possible at the time. Every replacement was as bad as or worse than its predecessor, but this no longer applies.

History repeats itself only when the circumstances are repeated, but we no longer need to repeat the mistakes of the past. The tools and know-how needed to transform the system are now to hand. Genuine democracy is no longer an idle dream. Worldwide cheap communications, the Internet and other marvels make it impossible to suppress the truth. The transition is nearer and easier than now seems possible. When two or three nations take the plunge, the rest will quickly follow and give backward countries whatever assistance they need. Change that once took a thousand years could now be made in as many hours or days. The only change that cannot be hastened is educating a new generation properly.

Some nations are better placed than others, but basic principles would apply everywhere. A first priority is to know where and why we are going wrong, beginning with economics and economic practice.

"What sort of forecast do you want for your manifesto?"

ISSUES THAT MATTER MOST

Economics

Economics is not the science it pretends to be. A subject that has given rise to thousands of learned textbooks and provides lucrative jobs for tens of thousands of academics, journalists and others of their kind, can be summed up in one simple sentence, namely: *'We can have only that which we produce'* or, as was expressed more cogently by an American President, *'There's no such thing as a free lunch.'* Its objective in a real democracy would be to compare the efficiency of similar workers and enterprises and use this information to improve quality and efficiency and conserve resources.

Put in another way, the most important of all economic realities is that all costs incurred throughout the economy are paid by the consuming public. Government expenses, taxes, company profits, litigation costs and damages, insurance, free gifts, competition prizes, lotteries, you name it, all come out of our pockets. There is no one else who can or will pay. The only difference is that the very rich get back most of what they pay, including tax avoidance fees.

Theoretical Economics

Theoretical economics has much in common with legal training. Law students learn how to make laws so complex and incomprehensible that only astute lawyers can find their way through the maze and find loopholes to avoid taxes and enable criminal to escape the law and devise ways and means of hiding the truth and making lies appear to be true. Economics students learn how to make simple economic realities so complex and incomprehensible that it is impossible for the masses to know the truth about the economy, government spending, taxation, public health, education and other important issues. Governments can then publish statistics that make even the most criminal policies look good.

GDP

Gross Domestic Product (GDP or GNP) is a typical example. This originally listed the nation's output of goods and services by volume and value, making it easy to compare one nation's economy with that of any other, but the disastrous effects of government economic policies compelled politicians to conceal the truth. The definition was therefore changed and GDP or GNP is now the nation's collective income.

Salaries, transfer fees, sponsorship royalties, prizes and management and legal costs of footballers, golfers and other sports people are classified as gross domestic product, and yet they produce nothing tangible. This applies also to revenues from sports and other entertainment, the colossal earnings of film, stage and pop stars, the royalties from patents and copyright, the excessive costs of advertising and commercial broadcasting, the profits from currency speculation, stock exchange dealing, money lending, financial advising and countless other non-essential services. The services we need most could be had for a tiny fraction of their present cost.

But there is another criminal reason for changing the definition of the Gross National product. The Chancellor of the Exchequer can pretend that taxes are a much smaller proportion of our income than is stated in government statistics and is constantly repeated by politicians.

Our brilliant and honourable economists appear to have ignored the fact that the nation's income includes virtually all government spending and that nearly all of this ends up as domestic income of one kind or another. The proportion taken of the nation's real pre-tax income is therefore much larger than claimed, an oversight that cannot possibly be accidental. The Chancellor and his colleagues could not get away with this fraud without their conniving. The declared figures should clarify the situation.

Taxes amounting to nearly £400 billion in the year 2000 were said to be roughly 40 per cent of the nation's income of around £1,000 billion. But this figure included nearly all the £400 billion collected in taxes, the reason being that taxes are used to pay salaries and other costs, all of which are income at the end of the line. In other words, nearly £400 billion out of the stated national income was recycled money that should not be called income, having been counted twice. The real proportion of the nation's income taken in taxes is therefore not less than 60 per cent and would be so stated, if the original honest definition of GDP were still used.

Mark Twain's 'Lies, damn lies and statistics' in ascending order of criminality is truer today than ever before.

All is intended to distract attention from the corruption of the present system and concentrate the nation's wealth in the hands of the system's controllers.

The British people are now frontline victims of legalised theft and deceit on the grandest scale. The per capita production of useful goods and services is made to appear bigger than that of Italy, much the same as that of Germany and France, and nearly as big as Japan, Sweden, Norway and Finland. It is actually much smaller than in any other European industrialised country and could be less than one tenth of Japan's, if GDP is defined correctly.

The fraudulent definition enables eminent economists to claim that London's £75 billion GDP is as large as that of Russia and Saudi Arabia and that it is larger than those of Thailand, Finland, Greece and Portugal! Britain's economy is said to be the fourth biggest in the world, larger even than that of China (*The Times*, 26 March 1998)! What is not mentioned is that most British workers are employed to provide unwanted or immensely overpriced services of one kind or another, whereas most workers elsewhere produce useful products, and that wages and salaries in different countries can be up to one hundred times more for doing the same job.

Economic deception is now practised everywhere, as evidenced by US national statistics for the summer of 1988. The stated unemployment was 7 per cent. Not disclosed was that 45.3 per cent of New York, Detroit and Baltimore residents over the age of sixteen were excluded because of poverty, lack of skills, drug use, apathy or other problems, and that non-accountables for the nation as a whole were 34.5 per cent (*The Politics of Rich and Poor* by Kevin Phillips). If the millions of early retired people and part-time workers who would prefer to work full time are included, US unemployment could be more than 50 per cent.

Old Economy and New Economy

Old economy and new economy are recent additions to the vocabulary of economic terms and further proof that economics teaching is not as it should be.

49

Old economies produce the tangible necessities of life.

New economies (increasingly referred to as 'empty economies') provide the largely unnecessary and immensely overpriced services.

Financial services should be viewed as 'oil to lubricate the machinery of productive enterprise' and should provide relatively few jobs.

Rewards in the upper levels of banks and other financial institutions and many other service industries are out of all proportion to the contribution to public well-being. The clerical and other workers who carry out the essential everyday functions are worse paid than ever before. Branch managers are ciphers. Job security for all but those at the very top is non-existent. The lower orders must rely on statutory severance pay when handed their redundancy letters. The top brass can collect millions of pounds, even if they are fired for incompetence. Members of the establishment win whatever happens.

If everyone were properly educated, earnings of trades, professions and other activities would be much the same for similar training time, effort, competence and experience. This was standard practice in the armed forces in wartime. Initiative and enterprise were not affected when the chips were down.

Another major benefit is that one wage earner could provide for the entire family. Mothers could keep house and care for their children until they are self-supporting without hardship or sense of inferiority, if they so chose.

Useless jobs are increasingly created to take people off the streets or make them feel they are contributing to society. A commercial enterprise is valued not by the contribution it makes to public well-being or its intrinsic value, but by its ability to make money by ways and means that would not be tolerated in a democracy.

One could well ask: 'What will happen to those companies when patents and copyright no longer generate royalties and all knowledge is free?'

They will be worth what their assets will fetch on the open market. Investments in high technology communications and information service industries will be worth much less, productive industries will be worth a great deal more. Statistics will mean what they say. Improving the economy's efficiency will be made easy. Nearly everyone would eventually be very much better off than they are now.

Another inspired 'misunderstanding' is the true meaning of 'money'.

Money

Money is not wealth, unless it is gold, silver or other precious metal. It is a means of valuing and exchanging different kinds of wealth and is worthless if no wealth is available. If fishermen stop fishing, we must go fishing ourselves.

All nations now have their own currency, although another that is more acceptable or stable than their own may be used for foreign trade or other transactions. Its exchange value, relative to other currencies, is fixed and periodically adjusted by government and banks, but this may not be its true economic value. This is determined by the efficiency of the economy and value of the nation's resources, and may not be reflected in quoted prices for days, weeks, months or even years. The difference between the exchange value and true value has created a major industry that is mostly legalised theft on the grandest scale, as is trading commodities before they are produced.

Buying and selling currencies or commodity 'futures' diverts wealth from the general public and productive industry into the pockets of large speculators who can manipulate currency and commodity prices. Huge profits are made at the expense of taxpayers (they make good the losses incurred by governments) or at the expense of consumers (increased bank charges make good the losses incurred by banks, higher prices make good the losses incurred by industry).

But the purpose of pretending that money is wealth in its own right, and that it is a commodity like any other that can be bought and sold for profit, is intended to do much more than make currency speculation profitable. By making money the primary purpose of every activity, even if the prospectus says otherwise, so-called 'New Economy' industries can be established to make immense profits by providing services that would be far better and cheaper in the society here outlined. They would also be immeasurably simpler and more effective. Best of all is that they would be free for everyone to use and would consistently and rapidly improve.

Free Trade

Free trade is an outstanding example of the way changing times can demand drastic change. It made an immense contribution to economic and social progress until large-scale mass production was transferred from high-wage to low-wage economies. Global markets became global suicide. The waste of human resources and the resulting misery are incalculable.

How can manufacturers compete with overseas producers, whose workers are much cheaper, more disciplined and better trained? The 1993 average hourly rates of pay (in US currency) were 44 cents in China, $24.98 in Germany, $16.40 in the USA, and $12.37 in Britain! Indian tea pickers may get less than the equivalent of US $1 per day!

The remedy lies in making all economies as diversified as possible. Given a suitable climate and sufficient population, any industrialised nation with sufficient farmland could produce the greater part of its food and manufactures. Exports and tourism would pay for essential imports. Consumers could be given greater choice by imports paid for by exports of similar products. Smaller nations could join like-minded neighbours. Developing countries would get free aid.

But no matter how poor the nation, the real incomes of its workers and their buying power would rise in line with improving education, more skills and the endless economic opportunities that stem from growing self-sufficiency. More evenly spread technology would eventually create a sustainable balance throughout the industrialised world, for technology is power. It must, however, be clearly understood that the essence of technology lies not in assembling components, but in designing and manufacturing the equipment and machines that make the components and the equipment used for their assembly.

Multinationals would no longer transfer manufacturing industries from high-wage to low-wage economies. Governments would encourage them to establish joint ventures with local industrialists with the aim of achieving the industrial diversity that goes hand in glove with a good system of education, now that nearly all technology can be efficiently exploited in relatively small undertakings. Small cost differences become irrelevant when workers are well paid. People who earn more can spend and pay more.

But it is important to understand that there are two kinds of multinationals. One produces the material resources needed for a good life, the other provides entertainment, financial services, media and well-advertised trivia. These last are made mostly in overseas factories where a day's wages may not buy a litre of milk! Packaging and advertising could cost a thousand times more than the content. Producers of the things we need most have yet to learn that cheap labour is suicidal in the long term and that independence through self-sufficiency is much more profitable. The more we produce, the more we earn for making them, the more we spend, and the more profit there is for multinationals and dependent businesses. Workers everywhere should produce goods and services to improve their own living standards and quality of life, no longer pauperising workers in 'rich' countries and making 'fat cats' rich.

Irrigating deserts, restoring lost rain forests, replanting lost forests, providing cheap water and energy-producing installations for backward countries are but a few of the countless profit sources that are as yet untapped. All that is needed is to use manpower efficiently and sensibly, employ only essential parasites, and pay those who produce life's essentials and wholesome luxuries what they deserve. The result would be an end to mythical booms, recessions, long-term unemployment, and the cruel exploitation of farmers, labourers and industrial workers.

The essential need for change is illustrated by the vast gap between the earnings of workers below top executive levels and the estimated revenue from sales of microchips produced in Intel's Israeli factory in the year 2000.

Published figures show that the average annual cost per worker, inclusive of all taxes and social security charges by the state, is not more than $30,000. Material and energy costs and overhead expenses might raise this to $90,000 at the very most. The budgeted revenue per worker is $300,000!

Distribution

Distribution may be the greatest source of waste after education. Present-day profit margins cannot be justified, even if every possible allowance is made for the costs incurred. Far more is now charged for selling a product than it cost to design, produce and deliver. Packaging can cost many times more than the content. Advertising can double or treble prices. Fewer and fewer distributors give buyers enormous power. Profit margins of small farmers and manufacturers are being reduced to virtually nothing, while prices continue to rise. More and more is spent on promoting brand names and increasing profits, all at the expense of consumers.

The potential for reducing prices is highlighted by the comparing the itemised production cost of video games with their £45 retail price in 1995:

Production cost (less than one quarter was wages)	£3.50
Royalties	£3.80
Advertising and marketing	£4.21
VAT (sales tax)	£6.70
Selling costs including profit	£20.15
Returns and miscellaneous expenses	£3.83
Manufacturers' profit	£2.81

Disk prices could be cut by 75 per cent and the wages incurred increased fourfold in a completely open society. Much the same would apply in telecommunications, public transport, energy supplies and other so-called 'utilities', all of which would be publicly owned and integrated.

Consumers would have constantly improving products and services at prices everyone can afford. Workers would be paid what they are worth. Electronic communications could be charged to taxpayers, like government and education.

It must, however, be clearly understood that distributors are not entirely to blame. Distribution costs, in Britain especially, are enormously increased by more government rules and regulations, higher rents and rates and other expenses than elsewhere, and by pilfering. Another is the sale of franchises and oil and gas exploration rights by government to the highest bidders, regardless of the added cost to consumers. Consumer protection is excessive and strictly enforced. Everything conspires to make end products and services as costly as possible.

But whereas distributors can recoup all their costs, being free from overseas competition, manufacturers are less fortunate.

Manufacturing Industries

Manufacturing industries in Britain have suffered more than in any other country. Appalling education, shortage of skilled workers and a mass of rules and regulations to protect jobs and so-called workers' rights have made it impossible for large-scale British manufacturers to compete with overseas manufacturers, even in countries where wages and salaries are much higher, as in Germany and Scandinavia. More and more factories, in Britain especially, are highly automated assembly plants that are owned by overseas multinationals. The machinery, equipment and technology are mostly imported.

These 'investments in British industry', so beloved of politicians and so highly regarded by the media, would more aptly be described as 'screwdriver factories'. Most workers are poorly educated, unskilled other than in simple assembly work. Pay is usually much less than they are worth, even when these factories are producing immensely profitable munitions and drugs. The economy as a whole produces very few goods and services that contribute to a good life. Those that do make life better would be produced far cheaper, were our affairs well managed.

Competition

Competition, as we now know it, is not needed when everything is open and above board. Openness is by far the most effective cost reducer in all things.

Professional Charities

Professional charities would be prohibited in a real democracy. Ample resources would be available for all worthwhile needs. Charity workers would be better employed and at far higher wages or salaries.

Insurance

Insurance would be a national responsibility with uniform premiums throughout the country, and with all claims settled by inexpensive arbitration. Coastal erosion, land settlement, storm damage, floods and other so-called acts of God would be government responsibilities, as would claims for injury from professional negligence. Proven neglect, however, would be severely punished. The potential savings are enormous.

Patents and Copyright

Patents and copyright would still be registered, but they would be free for anyone to use, other than to identify different brands. Their main purpose would be to identify the originators and award them the recognition they deserve. Inventors, designers, authors, composers, musicians, sculptors, artists and others who presently rely on royalties for all or most of their income would be generously paid full-time or part-time salaried professionals.

The general public would be encouraged to submit good ideas for consideration and further development, with international and national prizes awarded for outstanding contributions. Rejections would have full explanations.

Research

Research is a world leader in the league of wasters, but the inherent waste of secretive research is secondary to its potential for destruction and highlights the absolute necessity to outlaw secrecy in all matters than can affect other people's lives. Research, as now conducted, is the greatest of all threats to human survival.

Biological and nuclear weapons could not be developed in a completely open society. Nor would drugs that weaken the immune system and make us increasingly dependent on evermore powerful drugs, wheelchairs, walking frames, surgery and other medical 'marvels'.

All research and design establishments would be funded by government and fully integrated, their common aim being to improve living standards and quality of life. Targets would be clearly defined. Research or design projects would be duplicated in selected establishments in different countries. Findings would periodically be compared and made freely available. Outstanding achievements would be generously awarded. The result would be constantly improving methods of producing useful resources of every possible description, matched by better quality and design. The useful output of research staff would be several times larger than at present as they would all have a common purpose and would no longer need to spend most of their time and effort getting round existing patents, or finding alternative methods of doing the same thing, for no reason other than to make profit at public expense. New and better products would be made available when they were fully developed. Obsolete stocks would be recycled or given free to developing countries.

Energy

An immediate priority would be cheap, safe and abundant renewable energy, low-cost nuclear energy being the obvious choice if it can be produced safely. In the light of experience it is reasonable to suppose that co-ordinated international public funded research would achieve this within the next decade, but all other possible sources would meanwhile be researched simultaneously.

Munitions

Munitions production leads the world in creating waste of the worst possible kind. A common theme of British post-war trade ministers was that our traditional industries should be transferred to developing countries, leaving Britain free to concentrate on high technology.

They somehow forgot to mention that the technology they had in mind would produce immensely profitable munitions at a time when there were no foreign enemies and when their only buyers would be despots.

Or that the politicians and bureaucrats who determine foreign policy, negotiate defence contracts, license arms exports, create the demand for munitions and negotiate their sale are obeying the orders of their masters.

Or that manufacturers of weapons give clients and useful intermediaries enormous bribes disguised as legitimate gifts or transactions.

Or that most munitions sold overseas are eventually paid for by consumer goods produced by underpaid workers and that every worker making munitions destroys up to ten jobs of fellow workers in other industries.

Or that this policy would virtually destroy Britain's large-scale consumer product manufacturers, eliminate the need for skilled workers and create more parasites, frustration, crime and unemployment.

Or that the eventual outcome would be such chaos that the general public would welcome Big Brother societies, believing them to be the only way to abolish fear, terrorism and pending catastrophe and restore law and order.

No outsider knows the true size of munitions industries. Misleading statistics hide the truly important areas to which public attention should be drawn. For example, if a product is used 99 per cent for military purposes and only 1 per cent for peaceful ends, it will almost certainly be listed as non-military. It follows that even the most reliable statistics produced by the Stockholm International Peace Research Institute (SIPRI) may seriously understate munitions production.

The 1989 report showed US weaponry production to be 9 per cent of the GDP, with a further 1 to 2 per cent unrecorded, but everyone knows that immense quantities are also falsely labelled. It follows that as manufacturing accounted for 22.5 per cent of GDP, more than half of American manufacturing was munitions. Much the same applied in Britain, where even more sales were unrecorded and falsely labelled by exporters. Manufactures were 20 per cent of GDP, recorded weaponry production was 7 per cent of GDP. Britain is so dependent on munitions that exports for 1992 representing one-twentieth of world trade included one-fifth of the *stated* global sales of munitions. And all this is at a time when there are no foreign enemies!

Nuclear Weapons

Nuclear weapons are a deadly threat, but it is doubtful if they will ever be used on a large scale. World leaders are not suicidal. Nevertheless, we must be made to believe that a nuclear war can happen because nuclear weapons are immensely profitable.

Global demand for all munitions is now declining, despite religious and ethnic wars, but space research is making good the shortfall in profits. Good sense dictates that this should be deferred until the vast accumulation of past neglect has been made good.

Farming

Farming, as presently conducted, is a major source of yet another kind of waste. Everyone now knows that organic food is healthier and tastes better, but it is too expensive at present for most consumers, The demand is too small to justify the necessary investment in labour-saving machinery. It may always cost more than food that so often has residues of chemicals and toxic sprays, but the economic and social benefits would immeasurably outweigh the additional cost.

Many more workers would be employed. Yields, quality and public health would improve. Crops would be more diversified. Food imports would be reduced. Machinery with huge export potential would be designed and built. New food processing industries would be established. Good agricultural land would no longer be taken out of production. Savings in pesticides, fertilisers, machinery and other expenses would partly offset the higher cost of organic food.

The much larger rural population would require more schools, hospitals and public transport, better roads, numerous leisure centres and many other desirable developments. These, in turn, would attract small manufacturing industries, creating hundreds of thousands of well-paid, highly skilled jobs. School leavers in rural areas could have even more career choices than city dwellers, but there is an even more compelling reason for change.

Plants extract carbon dioxide and nitrogen from the air, convert them into plant tissue and return the oxygen. Plant tissue left in the soil decays and enriches it. Organic farming returns more carbon to the soil than is extracted from the air. It also reduces or eliminates the use of chemical fertilisers and dangerous pesticides, the toxic residues of which enter the water system.

Universal organic farming would therefore reduce global warming,lessen river and ocean pollution and improve the environment. The more thought one gives to this issue, the more obvious is the immensity of the waste we now tolerate and rarely question.

Recent experiments indicate that growing organic food in factories may be a commercial proposition in the near future. Agriculturists in Israel have already achieved 1,000 times greater yields of vitamin-rich salad crops in enclosed environments with automatic planting, feeding and cropping. This could transform the economies and way of life in countries that cannot presently grow food.

The Environment

The environment is a potentially fatal world problem that can be properly resolved only when waste everywhere is reduced to the level at which sufficient resources can be allocated to make an impact. Nations now have neither the will nor the resources, bearing in mind that as much or more labour and energy may be needed to remove pollution than were used to create it. This must therefore await world democracy. The best we can do meanwhile is to reduce pollution wherever possible.

Traffic jams, bottlenecks and the resulting air pollution could be cut drastically by underground factories and offices in residential areas, wider roads, overpasses at busy junctions and easy access to motorways. Better public transport, smaller, fuel-saving motor cars, more underground railways, mini electric taxis in towns and cities and other innovations would effect further huge savings in fuel consumption.

Urban housing would no longer be built to meet short-term promises. Most homes would have a garden. Well-designed terrace housing in cities and other urban areas could provide all the required amenities without using much more ground than apartments. Gardening on any scale is a delightful hobby that brings people together, no matter how different their views or status, and so makes a useful contribution to the environment and life quality.

But pollution is not the only environmental problem. Population control is equally important. Restrictions may be necessary, if affluence and security encourage people to have too many children.

Public Health

Public health, as presently cared for, presents enormous contrasts. On the one hand there are wonderful routine surgical operations that would have been viewed as science fiction when I was a lad. On the other is the increasing reliance on man-made drugs and inoculations with chemicals or serums derived from dead and frequently diseased animals. All these are now known to weaken the immune system. They could destroy us if this continues unchecked.

Enormous damage was inflicted before the dangers became obvious, the reason being that our in-built resistance is such that the effects may not surface for twenty, thirty or more years. Honest competent medical practitioners and observant elderly people now know that far too many of us are being made old, crippled, mentally disturbed or otherwise diseased before our time.

We accept as gospel claims by doctors that miracle drugs and inoculations are a boon and blessing because they save lives, not knowing that for every life that is saved, hundreds of thousands of lives may be shortened and made more vulnerable. To make matters worse, far fewer lives would need saving if we all ate the right kind of food and adopted a sensible lifestyle.

Typical of the present medical system's inherent dishonesty is the use of animals to test drugs. The cruelty involved is deplorable and attracts enormous publicity. The far greater cruelty to mankind is suppressed.

Few people know that two grams of the drug scopolamin will kill a human being. Two hundred grams is harmless for cats and dogs.

Or that one amanita phalloides mushroom can kill a human family. It is a health food for rabbits.

Or that a porcupine can eat more opium in one meal than an addict smokes in two weeks and then wash it down with sufficient prussic acid to poison a regiment.

Or that sheep can swallow and safely digest enormous amounts of arsenic.

Or that sleep-inducing morphine causes manic excitement in cats and mice.

Or that one sweet almond can kill foxes, parsley poisons parrots, penicillin kills guinea pigs.

Or that these animals are most often used to test the safety of drugs before they can be certified as suitable for 'curing' humans.

Or that vaccines developed from animals can and often do cause crippling and/or fatal diseases.

Or that one thousand years of vivisection has not produced one cure for human disease, but has produced more diseases than anyone can count.

It would seem that the animal testing of drugs can be very misleading, to say the very least. A health food for an animal can be death for humans and vice versa. The only safe testing is on humans.

Hans Ruesch in *Naked Empress* describes the growing use of chemical drugs and animal testing for drugs as 'legalised massacre'. Its perpetrators are the international pharmaceutical cartel, working hand in glove with those who control the medical profession, politics, the media and law. All nations are targeted. They have succeeded thus far because the overwhelming majority of doctors, nurses, researchers and therapists believe (or believed) that synthetic drugs are all they are claimed to be. Nor can they be blamed. They practise what they are taught.

The cartel is now so powerful that its members virtually dictate government health policies and the content of medical textbooks. They also control medical practice and research, media information and all else that affects public health.

Researchers who disprove wanted claims are sacked or denied funds. Crippling or fatal side effects are concealed for years. Doctors who preach natural methods are hounded and disbarred. Evidence contrary to the conspirators' purpose is ruthlessly suppressed. Misinformation is the norm. The occasional death of a patient who takes a natural remedy is seized upon as evidence of the inherent dangers of alternate medicine, even though the cause is more likely to originate elsewhere. The tens of thousands of premature deaths due to the shortcomings of conventional medicine are ignored or excused. The hundreds of millions of weakened immune systems are unseen.

That we now live longer and that fewer infants die at birth are cited as proof that public health is better than in the past. The real situation is concealed by fraudulent comparisons and by suppressing crucial facts. Notwithstanding incredible advances in diagnosis, treatment and surgery that should prolong active, healthy living, public health is immeasurably worse than it should be and is still deteriorating. We should and could have the miraculous benefits of medical advances without the drawbacks. Physicians, nurses and other staff cannot cope with the demand that is created by the inherent failings of a system of medical practice that most people accept without question. The truths that matter most are ruthlessly suppressed.

In bygone days most people were worked to death before reaching middle age. The majority was poverty-stricken, badly fed or half-starved. The tuberculosis, typhoid and other deadly viral diseases that flourished in their primitive living conditions were virtually eliminated by better hygiene. They are now reappearing in more virulent forms because our immune systems have been undermined by inoculations, drugs and poor food and are now vulnerable to diseases that could easily be resisted in the past.

It is not generally known that degenerative diseases, such as cancer, heart disease, diabetes, asthma and arthritis, are rare wherever people eat only natural food, live natural lives and use only natural remedies when they are ill. Or that these should not appear until old age, unless through over-work or excessive stress.

All age groups, including infants, are increasingly affected. Life for a growing majority of elderly people is now prolonged by drugs, surgery, walking frames, wheelchairs and other aids, few of which would be needed if public health were as it should be.

This does not mean that all drugs should be abolished. Used sensibly and transmitted directly into the bloodstream safely, as one should take vitamins, they can be invaluable, bearing in mind that nature provides remedies for nearly all the known diseases and that these should be developed and used to the greatest extent possible.

Prevention by natural means is the only safe and permanent solution, but the measures recommended by our authorities leave much to be desired because this is not profitable for drug producers, medical practitioners and others with a vested interest.

This short work is not a health manual and references must be limited, but good health is so crucial for personal and national well-being that room must be found for a brief overview, before proposing significant and long overdue improvements.

The human body has miraculous powers of healing and recuperation if the immune system is kept in peak condition by an adequate supply of the natural vitamins, enzymes and other life-supporting substances to which we are accustomed by evolution. These are directly or indirectly derived from plants and invariably exist in immensely complex mixtures. Many constituents are not yet identified, but it is increasingly obvious that these increase the potency and safety of the mixture. It follows that a varied diet of well-chewed organic food would supply all the vitamins required by normal people.

Man-made substitutes may have the same chemical formulae as vitamins, but they are entirely different, having no enzymes or other supporting substances. They also have reverse optical polarity and are effectively drugs by another name.

A little-known crucial feature of nutrition is that the natural vitamins and associated substances required by the immune system, most of which are water soluble, are damaged or destroyed by digestive juices. Nature therefore so arranges matters that these are extracted by saliva when food is chewed and transferred into the bloodstream through tiny capillaries in the mouth. Oil-soluble vitamins, however, are best digested and most conveniently taken in capsules or made otherwise palatable. Doctors never disclose this crucial difference!

The immune system adapts in time to cope with the viruses common in any given locality, but mass migrations created such an infinite diversity of immune systems, each with different vitamin requirements, that prescribing vitamins is largely guesswork. To make matters worse, most vitamins now sold are synthetic substitutes that may have long-term side effects and may be dangerous in excess.

The need to know the truth about vitamins is made more urgent by the fact that more are needed now than ever before and even more as we grow older, as the immune system weakens with advancing years. Our immune systems have a fast-growing workload. They must now neutralise toxic substances in food and in the air, repair the invisible damage of unnecessary inoculations and excessive antibiotics and cope with the increasing stress of modern life. The logical solution is to give the immune system the greatest possible variety from which it can take what it needs and store or discard the others.

Only one substance, fresh royal jelly, the mother's milk of bees, provides this choice, the reason being that a mother's milk contains extracts of all her food. Bees eat nectar in which is replicated all the vitamins, enzymes, trace elements and other vital substances of the plant, all in their most potent form. Furthermore, each component of a mixture of natural vitamins increases the effectiveness of every other component. It follows that only small quantities are needed, but it must be taken correctly.

Observant doctors know that natural vitamins are vastly superior to chemical substitutes and that our being more or less prone to certain diseases would not materially affect our health or lifespan if the immune system gets all the nutrients it needs. We carry viruses of all the diseases common to our environment, but the immune system controls them until it weakens through old age, shock, excessive stress, poor diet, pollution, and/or the toxic residues and chemical additives now present in so much of our food. We then develop those diseases to which our heredity makes us most vulnerable.

Eminent US biologist John Innuzzi describes royal jelly

as 'a veritable powerhouse of vitamins'.

That royal jelly is a remarkable food is proved by the fact that female larvae fed normal bee food become bees that live for days, weeks or a few months. If they are fed only with royal jelly they become queen bees that lay all the colony's eggs and live for several years!

No reference is ever made to abundant research findings from many countries confirming the wide-ranging benefits of this miraculous substance. Could this be because it cannot be patented and its supply is unlimited? Royal jelly would be a cheap and essential daily food if health care were as it should be.

The failure to make the most of our inherent resistance to disease is only part of the waste inherent in the present public health system and is best illustrated by analysing British health care statistics. National Health Service managers' pay trebled between 1989 and 1994, while nurses decreased by 6 per cent. For every £1 spent on patient care, £3.64 was spent on administration, seven weeks of which provided one and a half hours of treatment. Badly programmed multimillion pound computer systems increase complexity and play havoc with efficiency.

Contrast this with pre-war times when most British hospitals were small and managed jointly by a head physician and matron responsible to an unpaid governing board. Administration costs, even in very large hospitals, were a small part of total expenditure. Present-day treatments demand far greater medical care than ever before, but few managers would be needed if everything were open and above board. A mixture of small general and specialist hospitals could then give the best possible treatments on demand. Local clinics staffed with general practitioners and qualified nurses could provide everyday care and routine individual emergency services that are now provided only by large hospitals. Osteopaths, chiropractors and acupuncture specialists would give manipulative and other badly needed natural treatments not available in general practice.

Better food and quality of life would steadily reduce the demand for physical and mental heath care and put an end to waiting lists. Fewer working hours would provide ample time to provide unpaid social services. Helping the sick, the elderly and whoever else needs and deserves help would be welcomed as a duty and privilege. More people could work and be active until they die.

One final proposal. Visitors from abroad, regardless of the reason for the visit or length of stay, should carry a certificate confirming that they are not carriers of an infectious disease that is not endemic to the climate of the country that they are visiting and which is certified by an acceptable authority. Residents have the right to be protected from such

THOSE WHO PREACH LOUDEST ARE THE WORST OFFENDERS

hazards.

Pensions

Pensions are yet another source of waste and could well be described as 'an antisocial lottery'. Few working-class people have adequate pensions. A shrinking minority is far better cared for than they deserve. A universal compulsory pension scheme would maintain established living standards for the entire population and allow people to work for as long as they choose and change jobs as they please. Funded by deductions from wages, salaries and a proportion of company sales, the capital value of each person's pension would be treated like other savings. The fund would acquire shares in quoted and unquoted companies at current market prices, the ultimate aim being full ownership on behalf of the nation, but without the inefficiency now inseparable from publicly owned enterprise. Management costs would be negligible. Savings in manpower would be very substantial.

Law and Order

Law and order is long overdue for a radical overhaul. Crime proliferates because laws are so complex, incomprehensible and full of loopholes that it is relatively easy for unscrupulous lawyers to frustrate justice. The law has become an extortion racket compounded by secrecy. Justice and fair play demand openness in all things.

Laws in a real democracy would be simple, honest and even-handed because all the relevant facts would be available. Disputes would then be settled quickly and inexpensively by arbitration. The result would be fewer and fewer lawyers, negligible waste, increasing prosperity and real justice.

In bygone days one could shake hands on a deal. Endless rules and regulations have created a situation in which

KIL PIGGS

INNER CITY SCHOOL LEAVER

lawyers must now be consulted at every turn and can charge as they please. Fees of £5,000 for a single day in court and £750 upward for an hour of discussion are commonplace! A ridiculous lawsuit can cost millions of pounds in Britain and fees, claims and settlements are even higher in America. 'Ambulance chasers' encourage people to make outrageous claims settled mostly out of court to avoid the huge legal costs incurred in contesting claims.

By contrast, fees charged in all professions would be set by impartial pay tribunals and would be much the same as industrial earnings, there being so much more talent in a real democracy.

But having made these points, one must bear in mind that secrecy's potential damage to society was immeasurably less in the past than it is now. A fraud can ruin thousands of people; a criminal armed with a small bomb could destroy the life work of millions; a few terrorists armed with nuclear devices could hold the world to ransom.

Our misguided sense of human rights and sanctity of life causes many other problems, as is well illustrated by the way we punish habitual criminals and determine innocence and guilt. Crime can no longer be priced like groceries – paid for by a few days, months or years in a comfortable prison. Absolute proof of guilt in all circumstances is a luxury we can no longer afford. Proof of innocence may on occasions be as necessary as proof of guilt.

A very rare miscarriage of justice, with the victim usually a habitual criminal or associate of criminals, would be a small price to pay for a decent society and accepted like other accidents. But whereas major road, industrial or other accidents are newsworthy for a day or two at most, a questionable miscarriage of justice makes headline news for years!

The abolition of road transport would prevent road accidents. The closure of factories, fisheries, farms and mines would prevent industrial accidents. The closure of hospitals would prevent medical accidents. But we cannot live without transport, food, industries and medical care, and so we try to minimise the accidents they cause and view them as part of the price we pay for survival.

Law and order, too, is indispensable. Crime must be reduced to the barest minimum, if we are to prevent chaos and Big Brother societies in which ignorance, brutality and poverty are the norm. An occasional injustice is the unavoidable cost of a just and prosperous society, bearing in mind that the risk would be a thousand times less than it is now.

This greatest of all bargains is ours for the taking if:

- Legislation is simple, law enforcement is effective and withholding vital information prohibited, whosoever this may incriminate.
- Crime is not priced by fines or prison sentences that wipe the slate clean, penalties increase with every offence and

'THEY HEARD A RUMOUR THAT LEGISLATION WAS GOING TO BE ABOLISHED'

the evidence, background and circumstances of a criminal offence are thoroughly researched by a panel of three impartial lawyers on the basis of all the evidence.

- The alleged offender is tried in open court, given whatever advice is needed for defence and allowed to call his or her own witnesses.
- Every case is judged in the light of its own unique circumstances and appeal procedures are simple, speedy, scrupulously fair and irreversible.
- The police are incorruptible, efficient, dedicated to upholding the law and open always to inspection.
- We are all held responsible for our actions and diminished responsibility is rarely accepted as mitigation, even for homicidal maniacs, drunken drivers, alcoholics or drug addicts; parents are responsible for their children's behaviour.
- Repeated rapists and habitual paedophiles know they will be castrated and segregated, identity cards are mandatory, and proof of innocence is as necessary as proof of guilt, should guilt be obvious.

- Unexplained wealth is confiscated and disputes are settled by arbitrators.

Prisons would be self-supporting and run like commercial, competitive undertakings in which prisoners are taught useful skills, encouraged to acquire the work habit, treated firmly, but humanely and given tolerable living standards, good working conditions, normal rates of pay and adequate leisure. Working days would be longer. Earnings would pay for their keep, support their dependants and repay everything stolen or damaged, however long this may take. Intractable prisoners would get the treatment they deserve.

These measures have nothing in common with fascism. Everything in a real democracy is open, constantly scrutinised and modified when needed. Police could do whatever is needed to get at the truth, because everyone could see what is going on.

Narcotics Addiction

Narcotics addiction is now the most serious of all threats to organised society, being responsible for most of the nation's violent crimes, fraud, theft and premature deaths. The illegal production and distribution of addictive drugs is so easy and profitable that prohibitions and penalties are useless. Only democracy can destroy this evil trade.

Most people become addicted through ignorance, boredom, unemployment, poverty or peer group pressures. Once 'hooked', they will go to any lengths to satisfy their craving. Unscrupulous suppliers proliferate because raw materials are cheap; the bribes, fines and occasional 'hauls' by customs are pinpricks. Headline news of success is illusory. Published values are a thousand times more than they cost to produce. A tonne gets through for every kilo found. Convicted traffickers are instantly replaced. Drug barons are effectively above the law.

The only solution is to eliminate the profit by legalising drugs and make them available at prices that make illicit trading unprofitable, but with a three-pronged campaign to reduce and eventually eliminate the demand.

First would be a programme of education which stresses the enormous risks and disadvantages of drug taking, backed by well-equipped detoxification and rehabilitation centres in convenient locations. Second would be routine universal testing for drugs, with users required to attend approved centres until cleared, unless certifiable beyond help. The small minority unable or unwilling to break the habit should be fined or imprisoned only if they pose a serious risk to society. Third would be to restrict habitual drug users to menial jobs until they kick the habit.

Doctors would prescribe addictive drugs upon request, always reminding users of the risks. New syringes and reha-bilitation would be free. The only statutory drug-related offence would be to encourage drug taking, unless pre-scribed to relieve pain or other specific ailment. All social experiments involve risks, but few would be tempted in a prosperous, well-educated, exciting and harmonious society that offers a good life to all citizens and has effective deter-rents.

It is as well to point out that the most powerful opposi-tion to safe and effective liberalisation comes from the police, customs officials, prevention agencies and others whose livelihoods depend upon its continuation. Job securi-ty is all-important in our present corrupt, insecure system, no matter how useless or destructive. Immeasurably better jobs would be theirs in a real democracy.

The Media

Experience proves that those who control the media govern the country. It follows that none would be privately owned

POLITICS IS SHOW BUSINESS

in a real democracy. Newspapers and broadcasts would be more varied, intelligent and interesting. Pornography, unnecessary violence and commercial broadcasts would be banned. Bulletins and reporting would be comprehensive and free from bias. Constructive comment and criticism would be encouraged. Misleading reporting would be quickly and effectively remedied without recourse to lawyers. Journalists and reporters could no longer hound people or intrude on their privacy. Genuine rights and freedoms would be better and more easily protected.

A total absence of sensational trivia would allow much more space for cultural activities, education and the promotion of non-commercial worthwhile products and services. Press advertising would be simple, straightforward and devoid of sex symbols and hidden messages.

Newspapers and magazines would be fewer but immeasurably better to read. Less space would be devoted to advertising, more to issues and activities that improve the mind and quality of life. Why waste valuable time and space to advertise public utilities or competing brands of alcohol, soft drinks and unhealthy food? The media should help to make life better, not worse.

Foreign Policy

Foreign policy would no longer be dictated by munitions producers and large-scale industrialists. Revenues of poverty-stricken ex-colonies and oil revenues would not be wasted buying munitions to support despots and corrupt regimes. Native populations would no longer work for slave wages. Liberated ex-colonies would be freed in the true sense of the word. Countries ruled by despots would be compelled to become democratic by force, if need be.

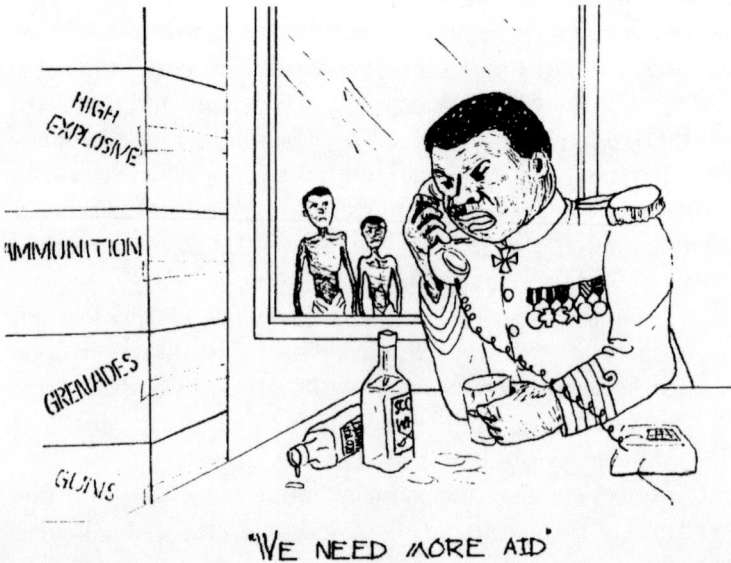

"WE NEED MORE AID"

Aid Programmes

Aid programmes would mean what they say and would be designed to improve living standards and quality of life, with nothing wasted on munitions. United Nations administration teams would oversee all government functions, train local administrators and implement totally free aid programmes designed to make recipients as self-sufficient and prosperous as resources allow. Efficiency experts would monitor their progress, cost and effectiveness.

Achieving economic parity with the industrialised world, while preserving the best of their own unique culture, could take fifty years or more, but the time and cost would be repaid a millionfold in human well-being. It would be the economic bargain of all time. There would be no more tribal or religious wars or persecuted minorities. Territorial disputes would be settled sensibly and peacefully by negotiation. Refugee and other relief agencies would be disbanded.

THE UNION SUPREMO VISITS HIS TROOPS

Trade Unions

Trade unions are not as they were intended or should be. Formed to combat the ruthless exploitation of workers by employers in the industrial revolution, British unions tried to reverse the situation and invented restrictive practices that made it impossible for industry to compete with overseas manufacturers. These eventually rebounded and they are now a shadow of what they were. Most trade unions elsewhere behave more responsibly, but all unions are in the same boat. Equitable bargaining is made impossible by mergers and a growing shortage of well-paid jobs. A new kind of trade union organisation will be the main instrument of government in the new system, as will be enlarged upon shortly.

Government Spending

Government spending has for many years provided excellent material for comedians and authors, but waste on this scale is no joking matter. Parkinson, for example, humorously showed that Germany got far better value for money than Britain in defence spending. For much the same budget, Germany's 1914 army was many times bigger and more powerful; her navy smaller, but better armed and armoured. Again in 1939, Hitler's army numbered millions, the *Luftwaffe* was many times bigger and more effective than the RAF, Germany's much smaller navy was better armed and armoured. Britain spent too much on top brass, red tape and administration; too little on weapons, combatants and training.

Excessive red tape and administration are still rampant, waste is greater than ever. Britain has admirals, generals and air marshals enough to wage a major war, and yet there are no foreign enemies. But this is not confined to the military. Legalised large-scale robbery of taxpayers is endemic in all public services, as evidenced by government contracts.

The proposed £1.1 billion Trident submarine base cost more than £2 billion. The Channel Tunnel, part private-, part government-subsidised, cost three times more than the promised £4.9 billion. The budgeted £164 million British Museum Library cost £511 million. The Thames barrage cost twenty times more than budget!

Everyone is protected by collective responsibility, the shield of rogues. Specifications omit crucial data, special requirements and other important features, none of which is 'discovered' until the work is too advanced for changes to be estimated. Contractors can then charge as they please.

None of this is accidental, bearing in mind the tools now available for tendering, and may explain why certain people who enter politics with little more than a worthless degree in politics, philosophy and bogus economics, a ready wit, a decent wardrobe and good connections become wealthy

"WE CANNOT AFFORD BETTER ROADS, HOUSING, PUBLIC TRANSPORT, MEDICAL CARE, PENSIONS, GERIATRIC HOMES..."

1900 GOVERNMENT SPENDING 15% GROSS NATIONAL INCOME

1985 GOVERNMENT SPENDING 50% GROSS NATIONAL INCOME

landed gentry in short time. Money need not change hands these days.

Expensive homes can be bought for half their price. Free holidays in luxury surroundings are theirs for the asking. Lucrative posts are found for relatives and close friends. People can be bribed legally in a million different ways. Are not election promises bribes? Dependency creates committed voters.

A family that has never contributed to society can get more in social security benefits than six pensioners, each of whom had worked hard for fifty years or more. A juvenile delinquent can cost British taxpayers £1,600 weekly to maintain in an institution, where he will probably learn the skills of habitual criminals. In 1998 newspapers reported a special home to house four delinquent children that cost £250,000 per annum. The average weekly cost of prison inmates was then £750, a figure that would be doubled or more if the costs of police, lawyers, judges, juries, courts of justice and the benefits paid to dependants are included.

The iniquity of the present system can best be seen if these sums are compared with the disposable annual income of a typical working-class family with two or more wage or salary earners. At the time of writing, this was probably less than £8,000, after rent or mortgage payments and other fixed charges!

Much of this appalling waste stems from an irrational public social conscience implanted by 'do-gooders' and is not confined to Britain. They now proliferate nearly everywhere and for the most part do extremely well for themselves by promoting these views. The social security income of an Algerian immigrant family in France (husband, four wives and twenty-four children) was reported to be the equivalent of £60,000!

Few people realise that all bribes are paid by taxpayers, or that government departments everywhere are over-staffed

and inefficient, even in super efficient Japan, or that Britain is top of the World League of Wasteful Spenders. Germany and France spend more, but public services are immeasurably better, surgical operations and treatments are available on demand, state pensions and social benefits are several times higher, roads are well maintained, railways are better and cheaper. But it is as well to remind ourselves that all nations are heading in the same direction and will stay on course until good sense prevails and we all opt for democracy. Government spending will then be as cost-effective as the best of private enterprise and will give as good or better value.

Taxation

Taxation is another area in which enormous savings can be made. Government statistics make it impossible to know how much we really pay and how much is wasted, but whatever the truth may be, both the amounts paid and wasted

THE PUBLIC SERVANT

would be very much greater if the word 'tax' is correctly defined.

There are two kinds of taxes. One is 'a levy by government to pay for the cost of government and public services'. In Britain this is officially claimed to be about 40 per cent of the nation's income, but this does not take account of the enormous sums collected in fees and fines that go into the Exchequer or are collected by local government. It is probably not less than half the total income, but whatever the proportion may be, it would be halved if useful manufactures and services were doubled without changing government functions or services. It would be halved again, or more, if government spending were reduced by more efficiency and productivity, full employment and fewer social security personnel.

The other tax is 'any enforced payment that is over and above the value received, regardless of who collects the money'. A lawyer's fee could well be 90 per cent tax or more. A Manchester United T-shirt sold for £45 could be an 85 per cent tax forced on parents by so-called 'peer pressures'. British railway and other public transport charges may comprise 50 per cent tax or more. All overprices are invisible taxes. British consumers pay more for motor cars, food, comparable clothing and other consumer products than consumers in mainland Europe or the USA.

Try to picture how much more could be spent where it is most needed, were taxes as low as they should be!

No one can forecast how government taxes will be levied in a real democracy, other than that the nation will get the best possible value in return for the money they spend in all areas of the economy. Goods and services will be the best that can be produced, sensibly priced and constantly improving.

Religion

Religion makes an immense contribution to a very different kind of waste, but, for reasons that escape me, neither its purpose nor the immense damage it causes are questioned publicly. Nothing is in more urgent need of a complete overhaul. One could well ask: 'Are so many competing religions necessary?' Or: 'How can so many people believe Biblical accounts of the Creation, of Adam and Eve, the Garden of Eden and other myths?' We know enough about the universe to realise that these cannot be true and that they were written in less enlightened days.

It is reasonable to suppose that there is a Supreme Power or Order, but religious beliefs should not dispute proven realities. Least of all should they be exploited ruthlessly and callously to create hatreds.

The Bible rightly preaches morality and mutual help, the very essence of real democracy. Religion should therefore be the root and branch of progress towards a better way of life. It could be, if we saw things as they are, not as present-day priests would have us believe. Conflicting versions of mythical fables, presented as indisputable facts by competing religions, serve the best interests of power holders by creating divisions that prevent democracy.

We can no more visualise and understand our Creator than ants can humans. No one can account for the random perfection of the universe, its immensity or its perfect balance. Typhoons, forest fires, floods, earthquakes come and go, meteors from outer space create havoc, and yet the environment is restored and goes on as before. Species that do not play their part in maintaining this miraculous balance disappear.

All living creatures, other than man, maintain balance instinctively from experience accumulated during millions of years of evolution. It would seem that everything we do or have done in the past is part of a continuous process whereby we learn from our mistakes. We should by now know that if we follow the example of all other living creatures, using our intelligence to make life better, not worse, we would make the best use possible of our talents and nature's resources and protect the environment.

Nature is best seen as an instrument devised by God to maintain a perfect balance, regardless of all other considerations, and is best described as 'random perfection'. Everything serves a purpose. The antelope eaten by a hungry lion is as innocent as those that got away. It served its purpose by being there, as were the tens of millions of peasants slaughtered by Stalin and Chairman Mao, the millions of Jews and gypsies who died at Hitler's hands, and the countless other innocent victims of oppressors. It would seem that we must know what is bad before we can know what is good. The mindless money-profit motive, ruthless commercial pressures, divisiveness and endless distractions hide the true purpose of mankind. Religion should open people's eyes to this purpose. We would then do what is right, instead of asking God to do it for us.

Religion is now big business and must share the responsibility for our woes. A good start would be made by thanking God, not for what we have, this being so much less than we should have, but for giving us the opportunity to make life very much better in the near future.

Which brings us to the final and most important of all issues.

Education

Education alone determines the way we think and behave, most importantly the way we bring up and teach children. Well-educated people would know how to make the best use possible of all the available resources. Most people nowadays

TEACHERS' STAFF MEETING

are clueless in such matters. The colossal waste of resources and countless other evils are proof positive that our system of education is not as it should be. Standards are falling everywhere. Every generation is less well educated than its predecessor. University candidates in Britain are known to have failed literacy and other tests set for eleven-year-olds, but all nations are targeted. Britain and the USA are merely front runners. People know much more about trivia and trash than in the past, much less about activities that contribute to a good life. Meaningless slogans and sound bites replace understanding. The authorities admit to many problems, but offer no practical remedy. The solution, as in all things, lies in nature.

Every living creature begins learning the facts of life from birth. Young animals romp, play and mock fight to develop body and mind as part of an instinctive process which teaches them how to fend for themselves. But whereas animals have no other choice, the system compels us to go against nature. Corrupt commercial pressures, fraudulently described as 'peer pressures', compel parents to undermine their children's physical and mental health and deny them a good education.

This must change. Our children represent the future. They cannot acquire the skills needed to sustain a balanced economy unless they are literate, numerate, articulate and healthy. They must also have enquiring minds and a thirst for knowledge. The rapid increase in our store of knowledge and the corresponding need for greater understanding create a situation in which education should begin earlier and continue throughout one's life.

Prominent educators differ about teaching methods. It follows that several should have extensive trials to see which works best. But whichever method is chosen, it must take account of the fact that the sooner infants begin formal education, the more they want to learn, the easier it is to learn more. Mental arithmetic, memorising tables, learning how to read, write, spell and punctuate correctly and speak fluently all give children the confidence, desire and ability to learn. Painting pretty pictures and playing with toys in school are complementary to this process, not a substitute. But what matters most is what they learn, how well it is taught, and the level of classroom discipline.

Age-old experience proves that children should obey knowledgeable elders until they acquire sufficient knowledge and understanding to know what best to do for their own future. With very few exceptions they would behave responsibly and need little or no enforced discipline. By contrast, the present system discourages learning, destroys discipline and instils them with little or no respect for their parents, their fellows and most other worthwhile things in life.

Every pupil should know that privilege is matched by responsibility, that we can have only what we produce, and that we should be paid what we are worth, as judged rationally. They should know also that we can have abundance of whatever is needed to live extremely well if everyone works together and shares the proceeds fairly, that happiness is not a divine right or commodity, and that the best and most lasting pleasures stem from fulfilment. Most others are transitory.

Good eating habits should be formed in infancy, with sugar, salt and sweeteners banned in infant foods. Sweets, crisps, fat-rich snacks and sweetened carbonated drinks should be occasional treats for older children only.

Foreign languages should be introduced as early as possible, with suitable subjects taught in a foreign tongue. A good working knowledge of two or more languages makes it easier to learn many more. Competition would be encouraged by periodic examinations, with prizes awarded for outstanding achievement. It may be old-fashioned, but it works.

Music would be compulsory. All children should be encouraged to play the piano and other instruments, aptitudes not being as decisive as it was supposed. Suzuki, the famous Japanese teacher who taught himself to play the violin as a child, devised methods that have enabled thousands of young children to enjoy music and become proficient violinists. Very few had a known talent for music. All children would be required to memorise good poetry, read good literature and engage in a variety of cultural activities, including mind-developing games such as chess and bridge. Ample provision would be made for sports, athletics, swimming and nature study courses.

The purpose of education would be to create a society in which people in all walks of life behave responsibly, are physically fit, can make a worthwhile contribution to society, are familiar with the best of our old and new cultures and can meet and fraternise on equal terms. There should be no class distinctions of any kind in real democracy, least of all on

WHO STANDS THE BETTER CHANCE?

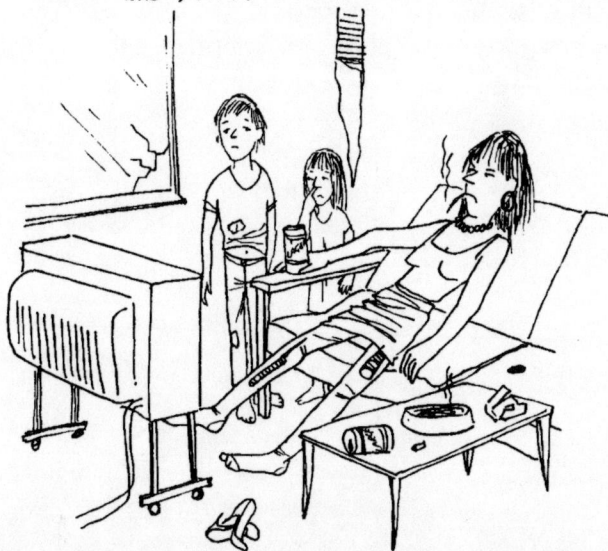

account of different standards of education.

Schools and colleges would have comprehensive indoor and outdoor sports and leisure facilities, staffed and used by local communities out of school hours. Funded initially by super taxes on excessive earnings in show business, sports and other non-industrial occupations, they could provide an endless variety of vocational, cultural, sporting and other leisure courses and a preferred alternative to mindless TV 'box watching'.

The syllabus for university graduates should encourage part-time work in industry. A two-year part-time stint doing unskilled jobs would foster financial independence and a proper understanding of economic realities.

Non-academic university students could choose apprentice-type courses combining practical industrial training and classroom theory, with proficiency recognised by an appropriate degree and ceremonial. Advancing technology, national self-sufficiency and the resulting far greater diversity of industry in real democracies would make careers in productive industry as attractive and financially rewarding as professions and service industries.

WHY ALL THIS WILL HAPPEN

WHY ALL THIS WILL HAPPEN

When one is brought up in a given environment and taught to believe that our way of life cannot be different, even if it is not as we would like it to be, it is extremely difficult to believe otherwise. For some people this is impossible. Indoctrination from childhood is the most formidable of all barriers to progress.

But experience proves that many of our most cherished and never questioned truths in the past were later proved wrong. Today's truth may be proved wrong tomorrow, whereas fundamentals can neither be changed nor concealed for ever. The facts will eventually speak for themselves.

Technology completely changed the nature and purpose of everything made or contrived by man in less than a Biblical lifespan. A world of unavoidable shortages became one that could give every normal person on this planet a good education and whatever else is needed for a good life. Long-established political, economic and social realities no longer apply. Politics and politicians have no place in a real democracy and will be consigned to history, together with the money-measured profit motive and other obstacles to progress, of which secrecy is by far the worst. Human nature is certainly not one of them. It makes us do what we believe is best for ourselves. The key lies in knowing what is best, and can be prevented only by universal ignorance. Internet and electronic communications make it virtually impossible to hide the truth much longer, even though the concept of a completely open society is abhorrent to those who are brought up to believe that the right to withhold information is the most precious of all human freedoms.

And yet the only losers would be politicians, large-scale speculators, lawyers and other legalised or unlawful criminals. Nearly all would be the last of their kind. Openness is the key to a world of justice, freedom, personal responsibility, prosperity and an ever-improving quality of life for everyone. Secrecy is now the only remaining obstacle.

That true democracy and its immeasurable benefits are no longer the impossible dream of a constantly improving world should by now be obvious. Granted that nothing man-made can be perfect and there will never be a Utopia, we can still have a world in which the quality of life constantly improves. All that is needed is a wide enough understanding of the fundamental realities of a constantly changing world and the determination to make the best of what we have for everyone's benefit. Our human nature will then perform miracles.

But nothing can happen before its time, nor can drastic changes be made overnight. This generation can at best see the beginning of real democracy, but we have a duty to our children and future generations. Our being poorly educated and unable to re-educate ourselves does not mean that we do not know the difference between good and bad education and that we should allow our children to be abused as we were, or worse.

It must, however, be made clear that every nation has a unique culture and way of life. The best features of these irreplaceable cultures must be respected and preserved without prejudicing the future. Measures required by one nation may differ from those required by other nations, but the following suggested proposals for Britain should be a good guide to those needed by most other industrialised countries.

But whichever these may be, constant revisions will be made in the light of experience. The rules will change yet again, when all nations are democratic and all natural resources are exploited for the benefit of all the nations. Change thereafter will smoothly conform to changing circumstances. Adapting to change, no matter how fast, is easy in a completely open society because the solution to any new problem is obvious.

A PROGRAMME FOR BRITAIN

The following economic programme is intended to make Britain once again a world-class producer of machinery and equipment with enormous export potential: a proud nation in the forefront of economic and social progress. The economy would no longer produce and depend upon munitions and worthless services.

It so happens that Britain's economic and social problems differ only in degree from those of other nations. The basic principles underlying these measures apply in all countries. Negative trade balances would in time become positive and used largely to assist developing nations and repair environmental damage.

- Establish a multi-purpose, government-funded trade union with the authority and resources needed to reconcile the conflicting interests of workers, employers, investors and consumers, giving preference to suitably qualified public servants.
- Withdraw from the European Union, restore traditional fishing rights in territorial waters and review all international trading agreements.
- Fulfil all outstanding contracts, including munitions, but make all transactions public. Convert weapon-producing factories to consumer products.
- Install regional and national databanks accessible by home modems attached to televisions and ensure that all information is accurate, updated daily and protected from interference.
- Establish the facilities needed to prepare and properly

present issues requiring decisions to the electorate, with all the known facts set out so clearly that these would always be in the nation's best interests. Regular meetings everywhere would encourage discussion and debate of matters of public importance.

- Ban imports of products that could be efficiently produced at home within a reasonable period, having first devised a mixture of incentives and penalties designed to continuously improve quality and choice. Early Japanese motor cars and other manufactures were ridiculed. They quickly became the best.

- Prohibit gambling in currencies and commodities and restrict money transfers abroad to the purchase of essential imports, tourism, business travel, and taxed profits (or dividends) for overseas investors until the economy is in good shape.

- Appoint panels of reliable industrial experts to evaluate the world's best consumer and technical products and select those most suitable for domestic manufacture. The nation's industries and farms must be as diversified as possible, the economy as self-sufficient as resources allow.

- Give loans and other incentives to approved manufacturers and experienced entrepreneurs to acquire the necessary machinery and installations, train staff, and produce a wide variety of competitive products for home and export.

- Encourage leading overseas producers to establish joint ventures with domestic manufacturers by guaranteeing a secure market, good profit margins (subject to quality and competitiveness with leading overseas producers), a good return on their investments, low taxes and an appreciating currency. The only condition would be that within ten years, the imported content, excluding raw materials, but including the machinery and equipment used, will not exceed 5 per cent of their ex-factory sales value. British manufacturers in the forefront of technology would be encouraged to establish similar ventures abroad.

- Set maximum profit margins for all industries that give manufacturers, farmers and other food producers, distributors and service providers a good return on investment, after paying good wages and salaries and providing for development and future needs. Powerful buyers could no longer compel producers to accept less than a fair market price. Producers unable to match the world's best within a stated time would be shut down.

- Establish regional offices, staffed with experienced management and technical experts whose function would be to monitor industries and professions regularly to improve quality and productivity. All services would be free.

- Ban pay increases not matched by cost savings until a rational incomes policy is established, but give employers and managers freedom to hire and fire as they choose. Redundant workers would receive full pay until they are re-employed, funded by a levy on wages, salaries and dividends. Lump sum severance payments and 'golden handshakes' would be abolished. Incompetent or negligent workers and managers would be downgraded.

- Prohibit restrictive practices and allow workers to do any job at the going rate.

- Set sensible pay differentials, working hours and conditions, health and safety measures for industries, jobs and professions and review these periodically.

- Restrict imports of fruit and other crops to those that cannot be grown, or are uneconomic or out of season, and give domestic food growers guaranteed prices.

- Compel all farmers to phase our the use of dangerous pesticides and artificial fertilisers and give them adequate subsidies during the five or six years it takes to transfer to organic farming. Agricultural engineers would be given incentives to develop equipment, specific to organic farming.

- Provide cheap energy to enable high value unseasonable produce to be grown under glass or polythene.
- All goods and services to be paid within thirty days from receipt of invoice. Bad debts to be reimbursed through a comprehensive credit insurance scheme. To issue a cheque without sufficient funds or buy goods or services on credit when insolvent would be a criminal offence.
- Limit stressful jobs, such as that of air traffic controllers, to five years and retrain them for less stressful work without losing pay or benefits.

Pay differentials would reflect learning time, skill, effort, danger, stress, job satisfaction, security and other relevant factors. The highest after-tax remuneration would rarely be more than three or four times the average. This, in turn, would not be more than two or three times that of the lowest paid competent wage earners. Special arrangements would be made for the partly or totally disabled.

Wartime experience proved that ridiculously high salaries and bonuses are not necessary to get the best out of top people. The modest and similar pay of surgeons, doctors, dentists, lawyers, accountants and other professionals in the armed forces did not affect their performance, inventiveness or job satisfaction.

We are engaged in the much more deadly war to preserve civilisation, end injustice and create an ever-improving world. Far greater sacrifices would be justified, and yet none is called for in the long term. All but a privileged few would eventually have a far better life. Within a few years the minimum take home pay would increase fourfold or more, bringing top after tax earnings to £250,000 or more at present-day values, with possibly as much again in bonuses.

Disposable incomes would increase even more, firstly, because the benefits of increased productivity would be shared equitably by the entire population; secondly, because money would steadily increase in value and have much greater buying power; and thirdly, because so much less would be spent on worthless trash and unnecessary services. Redundant workers would learn new skills in cost-effective training centres. Merit rewards and other incentives would go to those who make most progress.

CONCLUSION

The transition from primeval hunter to modern man has been marked by long periods of stagnation or negligible progress, interrupted by sudden leaps forward, none of which could be anticipated at the time. The former became shorter and shorter, the latter longer and higher. Technology is now said to double each year, and yet the average person is so poorly educated and so falsely indoctrinated that he cannot believe that the system can and will be immensely improved. Bearing in mind the potential of every normal brain to absorb knowledge and for people with eyes to see what is going on, this situation could well be described as the greatest negative achievement of all time. Only brilliant planning could create such widespread ignorance and apathy in the face of what should be obvious, even to those of us who are nearly blind.

Primeval man could not imagine horse-drawn carts, let alone atomic weapons or space travel. But having reached the stage at which there are no limits to productivity, and having developed and produced the tools required for real democracy, it should be obvious that all we need do now to create a relative Utopia is to educate our children properly. Only fools or knaves can dismiss this as impractical idealism or believe that this new way of life necessitates the sacrifice of personal freedom.

Knowledge in an open society gives everyone the greatest of all freedoms – to enjoy a full and infinitely varied life free from fear and insecurity. Our inability to see this confirms St Ignatius de Loyala's 'Give me a child for seven years and I will show you the man'. Indoctrination can be the greatest of all evils, with priests the worst offenders. Filling young impressionable minds with fables presented as indisputable facts is a deadly violation of human freedom. Sound moral principles should be instilled in a more enlightened fashion.

As one who finds peace and spiritual uplift in the solemnity and decorum of a well-conducted religious service, but whose feelings are summed up by 'I love the ceremony, the atmosphere of peace and the declared purpose, but I hate the words', I look forward to the time when religion will convey a very different message from those that now emanate from Bibles and most pulpits. The way of God will then become a reality and will be strictly adhered to in all activities.

It is admittedly very difficult for people who are brought up in any given environment to visualise what life is like in any other. Those of us who are accustomed to a stressful life full of contrived complexity, fears, distractions and false promises, or who are dependent on government handouts, are least likely to believe that any other way of life is possible. More and more feel helpless and trapped without the slightest hope of escape, and yet although nothing can be perfect or to everyone's liking, a positive and acceptable solution of even the most difficult man-made problem is simple when the cause is known and if the resources needed to resolve it are available. All the resources needed could now be produced if we so choose. Only the required understanding through education is missing.

No one knows what the future has in store, other than that there will always be simple, logical and practical solutions to whatever man-made problems may arise. Those who make economic forecasts are fools or rogues. The only certainty is that lost jobs will be replaced by better jobs. Stock exchange and other financial losses, no matter how immense they may be, could be made good and even bettered in countless ways. The only precondition is that secrecy is prohibited in all matters that can affect public welfare, with violations punished so severely that the possible gain is not worthwhile. This raises hackles in our present environment, but openness would quickly become an unquestioned habit in a world of abundance.

Genetic problems are a very different matter. These cannot be solved without attempting to play God. At best they can be alleviated, but this should not be allowed to inflict unspeakable hardship and cruelty on the afflicted or on their helpers or on both. Misguided compassion, more aptly described as 'commercialised compassion', can be the ultimate cruelty. Contrary to common perceptions, euthanasia, if agreed to be necessary by a qualified panel in a completely open society, could be accepted as carrying out God's will. However, compassion would be better directed towards the hundreds of millions of normal people who are presently denied the good education and countless benefits of a well-managed, high technology world.

The ultimate lesson to be learned is that we must conform to nature and accept that attempting to play God will always do far more harm than good. There are strict limits to human ingenuity and conceit. We can make the best or the worst of nature. We cannot create better. Replacement hearts, kidneys and joints are miraculous achievements, but nothing man-made can match the genuine article. If mankind is to survive and prosper, we must stop trying to improve on God. Genetic engineering, be it of man or crops, is an attempt to divert the course of nature and must stop. Much the same applies to inoculations using animal serums and to drugs that can distort the reproduction process. Should these be deemed necessary, patients should be warned of the risks and of the absolute necessity to keep the immune system healthy.

Properly targeted and integrated research in a completely

open society would have little in common with current researches. The quality of life and the environment would constantly improve without ever reaching perfection, if that is what we want.

Every man, woman and child can help bring this about. That few of those who begin the process of transition will live to see the outcome and reap the full benefit is immaterial. The duty of every parent is to do the best they can for their children. It is now up to us. We ourselves are now on trial.

THE FACTS REVIEWED

Genuine democracy is not the false promise of politicians. All we need do is conform to nature in all activities and use technology efficiently and exclusively to produce whatever is needed to make life better. Problems would be quickly and permanently resolved whenever they occur. A few decades

"WE ALWAYS VOTE FOR BLOGGS, HE MAKES BETTER PROMISES THAN THE OTHER LOT"

would see a world in which every normal person on this planet could have a good and constantly improving life in a cleaner, healthier environment because everything generates more of its own kind.

Openness in all things makes this easy and inevitable. All the information needed to do what is best for the majority is readily available to those who wish to participate in the democratic process. In short, technology plus complete openness destroys all limits to human aspirations and endeavour. Bogus democracy, by contrast, prevents our seeing this potential.

A list of the more obvious benefits that would stem from the transition to genuine democracy provides a fitting end to this work. It should be mulled over carefully until its many messages are properly absorbed. Others which should be included or have been overlooked may then come to mind.

Fewer problems, more personal responsibility and abundant resources would substantially reduce the need for government decisions. Education would make the most of our inherent ability. Nearly everyone would be literate, numerate, articulate, cultured and capable of acquiring the skills needed in a high technology society. They would also have a good grounding in music, the arts and wholesome cultural and leisure activities that improve both mind and body. These are essential to compensate for technology's constantly increasing mental demands and the immense reduction in physical effort, now that machines can move mountains and extract minerals from mines.

The free exchange of knowledge made possible by the abolition of restrictive patents and copyright would accelerate both the growth of technology and the restoration of the natural environment, bearing in mind always that removing pollution can sometimes consume more energy than was expended in its creation.

The economy would provide full employment, rewards

being proportional to the contribution each person makes to society.

Full employment would vastly reduce the demand for social benefits and welfare costs. Staff made redundant would instead be used productively. Working hours would be reduced across the board when output exceeds demand. Leisure time would be put to good use.

SHORTAGE OF STAFF

Maximising monetary profits would no longer be the aim of all enterprise. Profit would be measured by the increase in public well-being. Competition would be fostered by public recognition, by rewards for outstanding achievements, and by comparing like activities and publishing the findings.

All research would be open, integrated and international. Its common purpose would be to find better and cheaper ways of producing abundant, cheap and safe energy and whatever else is needed for the good life. Space research would be deferred until the entire world is democratic and the accumulated neglect of bad government made good.

Service industries would no longer be an excuse to make easy monetary profits by misinformation or legalised theft. They would 'oil the wheels of industry', provide constantly improving education, public health and other essential services, and employ the least number of workers.

Nations would join in the common purpose of cleansing and preserving the natural environment, reducing pollution and ending global warming. Water pipelines across national boundaries would provide all that is needed to remedy shortages and restore wilderness and deserts. Depleted rain forests would be replanted. Desert areas would be turned into forests, trees being the natural stabiliser of world climates. Threatened animal species would be protected. The environmental balance would be restored.

The abundance of talent that stems from a properly educated population and the openness that makes it easy to see what is best to do would combine to put an end to obscene pay differentials and deprivation. The lowest earnings of competent workers would be several times greater than they are now. The highest would eventually be no more than five or six times the lowest. All would have a lifestyle and quality of life that none could aspire to in present-day societies.

All nations would be as self-sufficient as their resources allow and would help one another as best they can. Third World countries would eventually be given whatever aid they need to become self-sufficient and democratic, and without any strings or debt. Despots would be past evils.

Productive industries would have an ample supply of well-paid workers with the skills needed to use the latest technology to the best advantage. Distribution costs would be a fraction of what they are now. Consumers would get very much more for their money. Farmers and manufacturers would be properly rewarded and could no longer be blackmailed by large distributors.

All published statistics would be based on honest definitions and would mean what they say. Economic growth would be measured by the increase in output of real wealth, not by the increase in income regardless of how it is earned. The economy would be described as booming only if it provides full employment and an abundance of healthy leisure facilities, while making the best use possible of all available resources.

Money would revert to its proper use and would no be longer a commodity. It would facilitate trade and measure real wealth, this last being defined as 'any resource that can improve living standards and quality of life'. Products and packaging would be designed to minimise waste and maximise recycling.

Mechanised organic farming would be standard practice. The use of toxic pesticides and chemical fertilisers would be limited to special situations.

The primary purpose of medical practice would be to prevent disease and premature ageing by natural means. Worn joints, heart valves, blocked arteries and other parts would be replaced or repaired without harming the genetic system.

Only natural remedies or substitutes that cannot damage the genetic system would be prescribed for fertile men and women. Most drugs would be derived from plants. Chemical substitutes would be used only as a last resort and always without risk to future generations. Genetic engineering and inoculations with animal-derived serums and/or chemicals that could harm the genetic system would be banned. Inoculations against foreign diseases, such as malaria, typhoid or a tropical fever, would be based on natural substances.

All highly infectious diseases would be notifiable. Sufferers would be isolated until they can safely mix with unaffected people. Intending immigrants or other visitors from abroad would be certified as being non-carriers of diseases that are not endemic in the countries they wish to visit or move to.

International telecommunications would be fully integrated and funded by taxes.

Openness would make it virtually impossible to cheat or commit a crime without being found out. Draconian penalties would make the risks not worthwhile. Honesty would be far more profitable than crime. An occasional, but very rare, miscarriage of justice would be accepted as the price one must pay for an orderly, crime-free society.

Narcotics addiction would virtually disappear without using enforcement agencies. Wars would be consigned to history. Munitions production would cease.

Minerals, oil and many other natural resources would eventually become public property and would be exploited for the benefit of the entire world population.

Surplus government revenues would be used to buy shares in all major industries at fair prices. Pensions sufficient to maintain living standards for the entire population would eventually be funded by industrial profits.

Taxes on useful industries would be phased out and replaced by taxes on consumers at levels adjusted periodically to meet changing conditions. This would put an end to tax avoidance schemes, complex tax rules and time-consuming counterproductive regulations. The personnel presently employed would be retrained and found better paid work in productive industries.

Sports would be divorced from commercial pressures. All sponsorships would be prohibited. Earnings would be much the same as for other skilled workers. Copyright could no longer be used to increase costs. Spectator sports would give pleasure without creating riots.

The general public would own far more worthwhile possessions and owe very little. Mortgages could be repaid within ten years or less. Credit cards would be used as a convenience, not to accumulate more debt and make banks rich. All credit card commissions would be charged to the cardholders.

Interest charges on loans would be very low because there would be no bad debts and the purchasing power of money would increase in line with growing productivity.

Populations would not be allowed to multiply beyond the level at which they would cause unavoidable and irreparable damage to the environment.

Charities would no longer be needed. Paid charity workers would be productively employed. Voluntary workers would have better things to do.

Disabled people would become fewer and fewer, but they would have the best help possible and be encouraged to contribute as best they can to society.

Religion would no longer create divisiveness and hatreds. Children would be taught the realities of present-day life and the need for unity and common purpose. All sensible people would know that the Messiah is not as portrayed in Bibles.

Technology used for the benefit of all living creatures must surely be the one and only true Messiah. It enables us to live as our Creator intended.

When what we now have is compared with what we should have, it will be seen that there is everything to gain and nothing to lose. It will also be made obvious that our leaders' consistent failure over the years proves that nothing in politics is accidental and that the cry of every sensible person should be 'No more politics please!'

Politics, politicians and career bureaucrats have no place in the genuine democracy that is now ours for the taking, given time, the necessary knowledge and determination. All we need do is wake up to reality, disregard the warnings of those who want things to stay as they are, and do what needs to be done.

Most people in Victorian times were convinced that it was impossible to provide an efficient public system of good water, drains and sewers for the entire population. More recently, no one believed that there would soon be space satellites, that man would land on and return from the moon, or that there could be an abundance of whatever we choose.

Nothing stated thus far is Utopian idealism. Genuine democracy will come when enough people know how to go about it. The impossible ideals of previous generations can now be realities.

Every effort should therefore be made to help those who clearly show they are determined to replace present-day bogus democracy with the genuine article, no matter how long or how much effort this may take. There will be no shortage of fellow supporters.

I will conclude by pointing out that exposing the failings of the present system is not likely to win Nobel Prizes, titles or lesser awards, but none could give me greater satisfaction than the knowledge that this book helped bring about the greatest leap forward in the evolution of mankind.